English Electric/BAC
Lightning

English Electric/BAC
Lightning

BRUCE
BARRYMORE
HALPENNY

OSPREY AIR COMBAT

Published in 1984 by Osprey Publishing Limited
12–14 Long Acre, London WC2E 9LP
Member company of the George Philip Group
© Bruce Barrymore Halpenny 1984

Sole distributors for the USA

Osceola, Wisconsin 54020, USA

British Library Cataloguing in Publication Data

Halpenny, Bruce Barrymore
    English Electric/BAC Lightning.—(Osprey air
    combat series)
    1. Lightning (Fighter planes)
    I Title
    623.74'64   UG1242.F5

ISBN 0.85045-562-6

Editor Dennis Baldry

Designed by Gwyn Lewis
Printed in Spain

TITLE PAGES
*Lightning F.3 (XP701/'A') of No 29 Sqn at RAF
Wattisham, April 1970
(Flight)*

Contents

Preface

After twenty-three years the Lightning has easily
become the longest-serving front-line fighter in the
Royal Air Force. It was not envisaged that this
would be the present-day situation, but then
circumstances one way and another have always
controlled the Lightning's destiny over these past
years. The aircraft since at least 1969 has always
had a series of end-of-service dates in prospect and
this has been the major factor in limiting some of
the necessary modifications that are really of prime
importance to a modern fighter aircraft, and would
have made the Lightning even more effective.
Thus has the Lightning been truly a hostage to
fortune, a thoroughbred fighter if ever there was
one, following on from the great names of the
past: Camel, Spitfire and Hunter. As fortune's
hostage perhaps it deserved better, but then
nothing is ever perfect. This book on the
Lightning is a veritable pot-pourri of information
on the aircraft from its conception to the present
day, the squadrons it served with, what it's like
from the pilot's and engineer's viewpoints, and for
the total enthusiast what has happened to all the
Lightnings that were ever built. From my personal
viewpoint, knowing that this book was to be
written has brought a great deal of satisfaction
because all of us who have been privileged to fly
this aircraft will never forget it. And to those who
come after us and will just see the aircraft in a
museum or as a gate guardian this publication will
bring the aircraft back to life in a way that will last
as long as men talk of one of the all time-great
aircraft – the Lightning.

Wg Cdr 'Mike' Streten
Officer Commanding
No 5 Sqn
RAF Binbrook, England
1984

Introduction

The Lightning was built for the RAF as a supersonic Mach 2 interceptor and in the 1950s plans had been made for Lightning deployment in the defence of the United Kingdom. Part of the programme was to bring up to operational status many of Fighter Command's airfields along the east coast. They had been selected as potential Lightning bases and their runways strengthened and lengthened to 7,500 ft (2,286 m) so that they would be suitable for supersonic fighters.

Then came the catastrophic 1957 Defence White Paper. Duncan Sandys, Secretary of State for Defence in the Macmillan Government, predicted that manned aircraft would be replaced by missiles. Subsequent defence cuts resulted in serious setbacks for the British aircraft industry and many of the airfields slated for the Lightning were closed or abandoned by the RAF after only a short period of occupation. Quite simply Sandys saw no future for manned military aircraft. All defensive and offensive aircraft could be replaced by 'cheaper' missiles. Axed projects included the Avro supersonic bomber, fighter and high-speed research aircraft such as the SR.53 and SR.177, Gloster (thin-wing) Javelin and Fairey Delta 2 derivatives. The Lightning was spared, but Sandy's ill-advised intervention was to have an adverse effect on the Lightning, for it withered its development and killed everything after it. A great pity, for when No 74 Sqn received the Lightning in July 1960 it probably had the best supersonic interceptor in the world. The Lightning was intended to be used to intercept high-flying targets as far out from the UK as possible, relying on fast reaction time (cold start to airborne 1.5 min), very high rate of climb and phenomenal acceleration. Initial rate of climb – over 8 miles (12 km) a minute—reaching 40,000 ft (12,195 m) in 2.5 minutes from brakes off. It can zoom climb to well over 70,000 ft (21,336 m). However, the penalty for thirsty engines and small fuel capacity has to be paid for and its range is short. The Lightning can cruise economically on one engine up to about 25,000 ft (7,620 m), and can fly on one engine up to much higher altitude. It is inherently stable over a 13:1 speed range, and can be flown hands-off and rolled at Mach 1.8 without auto-stabilization. The Lightning is easily supersonic using dry thrust only.

The early Lightnings, the F.1, F.1A and F.2, all had guns in addition to Firestreak missiles. Then came another misconception that the day of the dogfight was over. The Lightning F.3 was a more powerful and a more sophisticated machine, equipped with Red Top missiles. But no guns. The more powerful engines made the endurance of the F.3 even more critical, and an in-flight refuelling probe became a necessity—and the pilot still had to keep one eye on the fuel. It took many months before the gunless F.3 was handed over to the RAF.

By 1964 it had finally sunk in that the manned fighter was here to stay and increased development funding produced the F.6 Lightning with a much improved fuel capacity but still without guns. However, the Vietnam and Arab/Israeli conflicts had shown that a fighter without guns was at a serious disadvantage in combat. This prompted a re-think about the F.6 concept, and a gun was fitted in an enlarged ventral tank, which not only improved the Lightning's lamentable endurance, but also reduced drag and, as an added bonus, the fuel was used to cool the guns.

Throughout its long life the Lightning was always going out of service. From birth it was always short of funds because of the belief that it was to be the RAF's last fighter and would soon be replaced by missiles. Time has proved that this was not to be the case. Missiles form the final defence but they can never replace the manned interceptor. With increasing civil traffic and probing 'non-hostile' flights by Soviet aircraft the manned interceptor is the identifier for the ground controller.

With its superior aerodynamic performance the Lightning compares well with modern Soviet fighters such as the MiG-23, and not until late 1986 will it be replaced by the Panavia Tornado F.2.

When the supersonic Lightning was put into service in July 1960 it represented the total weapons system approach and was fully integrated into the UK air defence system. The Lightning is an enjoyable aircraft to fly and an effective weapons system, but tactics have changed – 'If you fly high enough, long enough, the enemy will always get you.' The Lightning can reach very high altitudes and successfully intercepted a flight of Lockheed U-2s. But now the war role calls for flying fast and low at Mach 0.8 and at an altitude of 250 ft (75 m). Pilots regard these heights as a minimum, rather than a maximum.

The Lightning is now dating and to keep it in service cannibalism, transplants, and incredible technical ingenuity is a necessity. Surviving aircraft have been rebuilt so often that almost nothing remains of the original airframes, engines or innards. The groundcrews curse it, but pilots love it even in its twilight years. It is a rare beast that one cannot help but love and admire. When the Lightning goes, gone also will be the last classic British fighter design. Gone will be the last single-seat fighter in the RAF. It was the only all-British supersonic aircraft to enter squadron service.

Bruce Barrymore Halpenny
Market Rasen, England
1984

Chapter 1
Lightning Evolution

The development of the Lightning goes back to just after the World War II when W E W Petter, then chief engineer of the English Electric Aviation Company, made a few sketches.

In 1947 the Ministry of Supply issued Experimental Requirement 103 (ER 103) for a manned research aircraft capable of exploring transonic and low supersonic speeds. An objective of Mach 1.5 at 30,000 ft (9,145 m) was set, this being more or less identical to that claimed for the cancelled Miles M.52 supersonic research aircraft under construction a year before. The following year ER 103 was taken up by two manufacturing firms: English Electric and Fairey. Both studied the requirement closely and in September 1948 the supersonic research programme began.

The Fairey delta-wing design was conceived as a pure research project and it became the record holding FD.2, virtually a minimum supersonic envelope for a pilot, engine, and fuel. The data from Fairey's aeroplane was extensively adopted for the development of the Dassault Mirage III fighter.

In contrast to Fairey the English Electric team under the leadership of W E W Petter—designer of the Canberra, Gnat, Whirlwind and Lysander—decided in favour of a rather larger machine, powered by two turbojets mounted one above the other and staggered, fed from a intake in the nose. Petter placed great emphasis on minimizing frontal area. The staggered engine arrangement ensured symmetrical thrust in the event of an engine failure, and cross-section area was reduced by about 50 per cent. The wing structure was passed through the fuselage between the upper and lower intake ducts.

English Electric's project team differed from Fairey in electing to use a heavily swept wing of moderate taper rather than the structurally simpler delta.

Basic gathering of data was the first task and various American agencies gave help with information on the stability, control and other problems of such aircraft as the Bell X-1, which reached Mach 1.46 at 70,000 ft (21,336 m) on 14 October 1947 and the North American F-86 Sabre, capable of supersonic speed in a dive and destined to achieve immortality over the Yalu

River in Korea. Incidentally, an F-86 had been flown at transonic speed in May 1948 by Wg Cdr E R 'Roly' Beamont, English Electric's chief test pilot, during a visit to Wright Field and he became the first non-American to exceed the speed of sound.

Naturally enough, English Electric felt that most of the work for which a purely experimental supersonic aeroplane could be built had already been done across the Atlantic. It seemed logical therefore to look upon the project as a basis for a fighter, and the company designed the aircraft to incorporate armament and other military equipment should this become a requirement. The designation P.1 was adopted for the project.

The English Electric proposal was submitted and the Ministry of Supply was sufficiently impressed to issue specification F.23/49 for a supersonic day fighter on 3 September 1949.

The project proceeded quickly on the drawing boards of English Electric as the team set about converting the project scheme into working drawings.

On 1 April 1950, a contract was signed for the construction of two P.1A research aircraft, in parallel with an intensive wind tunnel programme. English Electric developed the first company-owned transonic tunnel outside the USA by modifying an existing jet engine-driven tunnel to a slotted working section. This first ran at transonic speed on 20 July 1950, and a complete P.1A model tested during 1951 was displayed at the London Science Museum. The low speed aerodynamics of the P.1A layout were explored in the 9 ft × 7 ft (2.7 m × 2.1 m) wind tunnel and the 18 inch (45.7 cm) water tunnel at Warton, starting in 1949. The vortex flow arising from the early tip stall was inspected in water, and the high downwash angles in the high tailplane region were explained.

This gave confidence in the load measurements taken from the wind tunnel, and proved that a low tailplane position was desirable for satisfactory low-speed handling and to avoid pitch-up problems in the transonic region.

The original layout had a fin-mounted tailplane, a mid-low wing, and the upper engine mounted forward, above the wing. The modified layout moved the wing to a shoulder position, with the upper engine to the rear and the lower engine forward below the wing. Lifting the wing was necessary to get the tailplane sufficiently below the wing wake.

At this stage the Royal Aircraft Establishment came on the scene in its capacity as adviser to the Ministry of Supply. The RAE expressed their doubts about the unconventional position of the tailplane. The English Electric team insisted that if low-speed handling was to be acceptable then a low position was called for. However, the RAE technicians remained unconvinced and the Ministry of Supply decided to fund the construction of an aircraft for research into the low-speed behaviour of the English Electric design. Tunnel evidence had left little room for doubt about how the supersonic machine would fly, but the value of trials at Reynolds numbers appropriate to full-scale experience could not be denied. The task of building the research machine fell to Short Brothers and Harland. The resulting SB.5 was powered by a single Rolls-Royce Derwent turbojet.

The layout of this aircraft was such that it could have its wing swept to 50°, 60° or 69° and its tailplane mounted in the high, low or mid-positions. The SB.5, serial WG768, first flew with Tom Brooke-Smith at the controls in December 1952 in 50° swept wing, high tailplane layout

configuration. The wing was subsequently swept to the 60° position (retaining the high tailplane setting during 1953), and finally flew in the 60° wing, low tailplane layout in December 1953.

Wing drops were experienced on the SB.5 during early 1954, and tunnel tests at Warton suggested that a sharp leading edge or notches would soften the tip stalls. Both were tried in flight, and both were effective, the notches being favoured because they did not affect induced drag in the attached flow regime, whereas the sharp leading edge destroyed the leading edge suction.

These notches were adopted for the P.1A wing before it first flew, but after 95 flights the notches were filled in and it was proved that they were not necessary for low-speed flight. Subsequently it was proved that the SB.5 wing drops were due to the manual ailerons. However, the notches were revived on the P.1A for transonic reasons, and as a convenient location for the fuel tank vent.

English Electric's chief test pilot, Wg Cdr Roland 'Roly' Beamont at the controls of the first P.1A, WG760. The P.1A was little more than a supersonic research vehicle. Picture taken from a Meteor flying chase. WG760 served as a gate guardian at RAF Henlow from 1966 until it was moved to RAF Binbrook for restoration in 1982 (BAe)

The configuration proved stable and trimmable until the wing stalled, with no pitch-up over the whole flight envelope. In transonic conditions, of course, there was a very slight trim change because of the inevitable shift in aerodynamic centre when decelerating in the region of Mach 1.

A product of the complicated vortex flow associated with all highly-swept and tapered wings is high upwash and hence high local tip lift. Wing-tunnel investigation showed that a notch in the leading-edge at the right point, instead of the usual wing fence, modified the vortex and boundary layer patterns at the tip and eliminated this effect. Lighter, simpler and less drag-producing than fences, the 'saw-cuts' have been standard on all developments of the P.1, and have since been incorporated in several other aircraft.

Experience with the SB.5 confirmed the desirability of a highly-swept aerodynamically-thin wing, which was nevertheless thick enough to house a reasonable structure, the main undercarriage and fuel. The values finally selected for the P.1, to avoid violent buffet and trim changes in transonic flight, were 60 degrees sweep on the leading edge and 52 degrees on the trailing edges; with a mean thickness/chord ratio of about 5 per cent the wings were five-spar structures built up in two panels, joined on the centreline and skinned with 0.2 inch (8 mm) metal sheets to provide integral fuel tanks.

In its initial form, the aircraft was envisaged as a pursuit-type weapons system, using classic stern-chase tactics to position itself for an attack with cannon, air-to-air rockets or missiles. To reach jet bomber operating ceilings in the minimum time, and for the necessary acceleration to close on high-speed targets a very high power-to-weight ratio was required, which dictated the installation of two jet engines.

Area rule as such did not govern the final shape of the P.1 fuselage, although the wing/body combination conformed approximately to its requirements. Tests proved that the minimum combined drag was obtained with thin, highly swept wings combined with sensibly straight (rather than convex) bodies. Positioning the upper engine well to the rear of the lower allowed the area at the critical wing—fuselage junction to be as low as possible.

One of the next considerations was intake design. In the early 1950s, side intakes on various international projects were in serious trouble, and facilities in Britain for studying inlet development

A recent picture of the somewhat basic instrument panel of P.1A WG760 taken at Binbrook. Several instruments have been removed

were then limited. The intake was positioned in the nose to obtain the greatest possible efficiency and avoid disturbances from weapon launch, which are damped out in the resulting long diffuser duct.

Of the two initial P.1As, one (WG760) was used for handling and performance development, and the other (WG763) for structural research and armament development. A plain intake was sufficient for the low supersonic performance conferred by the two Armstrong Siddeley Sapphire ASSa.5 turbojets. These each developed 8,100 lb (3,674 kg)—later 10,310 lb (4,676 kg) with reheat. WG760 made its first flight in the hands of chief test pilot 'Roly' Beamont at Boscombe Down on 4 August 1954. The P.1A emerged as a singularly ugly but potent-looking aircraft, with a big elliptical and canted nose intake, and long Messier mainwheel legs retracting outwards into the thin wings, pivoting through 60 degrees in the process.

After accelerating to Mach 0.85 on its first flight, the P.1A went transonic exactly a week later, on its third sortie. It was thus the first British aircraft to exceed Mach 1.0 in level flight. In July 1955, the second P.1A, WG763, joined the flight-test programme.

The second prototype was something more than a research vehicle and differed from its data-gathering predecessor in that it was fitted with two 30 mm Aden cannon, plus some operational equipment and a ventral tank containing 250 Imp gal (1,136 lit) of fuel. A Napier Double Scorpion rocket pack was projected to boost the climb and ceiling of the P.1B. This rocket motor was demonstrated on a Canberra test bed, and the first Scorpion pack for the Lightning was manufactured, but the requirement was (typically) cancelled.

Both P.1A flight prototypes provided invaluable supersonic experience, and revised aileron and tailplane gearing reduced sensitivity. Different wing profiles were also tried out on the basic English Electric ASN/P1/3 section. Drooping leading-edge flaps on the inner wings were soon abandoned on WG760, but a more significant modification involved a cambered leading-edge extension plus wide-chord tips, also resulting in completely inset ailerons. This considerably reduced drag for subsonic cruise, and this increased the range and combat patrol time, and was of significant benefit in improving the take-off and approach handling characteristics.

Amazingly, the cambered wing was not adopted for initial production aircraft, but was revived for the Lightning F.6. Other development work on the P.1A included gun-firing trials in WG763, successful tactical evaluation by the Central Fighter Establishment, and extended pure supersonic research in the Aerodynamics Flight at

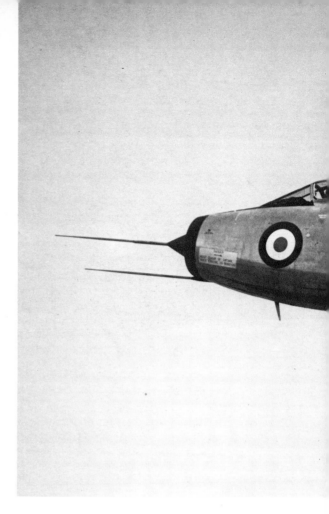

the RAE, Bedford. Having been conceived as a test vehicle for speeds up to about Mach 1.2, the P.1A was eventually pushed to a figure as high as Mach 1.53 (1,010 mph–1,625 km/hr). Handling was as remarkable as its performance on relatively limited power, and it proved capable of manoeuvring through its entire flight envelope without the aid of auto-stabilization, although this was naturally fitted for accurate weapon delivery.

WG760 and its sister ship WG763 completed more than 500 flights. The two prototypes were flown by Service and civilian pilots who found them completely straightfoward flying machines presenting no special conversion problems. Fighter Command was represented at Warton by Sqn Ldr James 'Jimmy' Dell, who flew WG763 over Aberporth and did trial runs with the radar-controlled pattern at the range. Most of the flying with the two P.1A prototypes was carried out from the company's airfield at Warton. WG763 took part in the SBAC Display at Farnborough in September 1955, the first public demonstration of the type. One should also mention here the third prototype (WG765) which never flew. It served at Warton as a 'breaking frame' for static testing.

While the P.1A was passing through the detail design stage it was generally accepted that future fighters would be hugely expensive and bought in much smaller numbers than their predecessors.

Powered by Rolls-Royce Avon 24R (Mk 210) turbojets with four-stage reheat, the first P.1B, XA847, was equipped with a conical fibreglass centrebody in the mouth of the engine intake with an instrumentation probe (no radar was fitted). In November 1958, XA847 became the first British aircraft to reach Mach 2 (Flight)

Moreover, it was generally accepted that there was little point in developing a complicated supersonic aeroplane for the defence of the UK unless the aircraft could operate at night or in bad weather. It is pertinent to record that, contrary to a decision previously taken by the USAF, the British Air Staff considered that the full requirements for all-weather interception could be met only by a two-seat aeroplane. English Electric felt that, as the ultimate aim was the elimination of the fighter pilot, it was logical to minimize the crew as far as possible and make automatic equipment perform all the essential functions of the weapons system.

Contractual development of the P.1A was only part of the original Ministry order, which also covered the construction of three operational prototypes, designated P.1B, and they were recognized as the true initial design of the new weapons system and were exclusively provided for power-unit experiments and armament trials. When Petter left English Electric for Follands, work on the project continued under the direction of F W 'Freddy' Page, then chief engineer of English Electric at Warton, and integrating the weapons system concept resulted in numerous changes from the P.1A.

Most extensive of these concerned replacement of the limited-thrust Sapphires by two Rolls-

Royce Avon engines (and subsequently by Avon RA.24R Mk 210s), described by Page as the largest, lightest and most suitable engines then available. The RA.24R has air-cooled turbine blades and ratings of 11,250 lb dry (5,103 kg) and 14,430 lb (6,545 kg) with afterburning. The 200-series Avons in the F.1 and F.1A did not have fully modulated afterburning, being provided with four reheat nozzle settings for fixed-thrust outputs. In the first reheat setting, however, thrust variation was possible by altering engine RPM.

With nearly double the installed thrust of the P.1A, the Avon-engined P.1B prototypes required a more sophisticated intake, achieved by installing a fixed conical centrebody. This simple two-shock intake, with no complicated bleeds or pressure relief systems, was evolved to provide a duct with high-pressure recovery and low drag, capable of operating satisfactorily over a wide speed and incidence range, while giving good distribution at the engine face and good throttle handling.

15

The fixed-cone intake of the type used by the Lightning and MiG-21 is highly efficient at subsonic speeds and is designed to give an optimized flow pattern at around Mach 2.0 by deflecting the shock cone outside the intake lip. In the transonic regime momentary choke is experienced, but the thrust reserve of the Lightning ensures that this only lasts a couple of seconds, and no consumption penalty arises. The resulting advantages from avoiding a variable intake are considerable, especially as the Lightning centrebody provides a made-to-measure and quickly removable pressurized capsule for the Ferranti Airpass AI.23 fire-control radar. The shock-wave system ahead of any intake can become unstable if the intake geometry and mass flow are not properly matched for the particular Mach number, and the resulting oscillations could give rise to the highly destructive phenomena of intake 'buzz'.

Other changes in the P.1B resulted in a virtually new fuselage, including a raised cockpit to improve the combat view and headroom, and a fairing in the new canopy with a dorsal spine. This was used to house additional equipment, including the iso-propyl-nitrate (Avpin) Plessey starter tanks and pumps. The lower strut support for the centrebody provided convenient stowage space for the nosewheel, which was modified to retract straight forward instead of pivoting to lie flat, and became non-steerable. The air brakes were changed in shape, and moved ahead of the fin to avoid trim change, and the split flaps of the P.1A were replaced by simple hinged surfaces. The Lightning is unusual, however, in using a substantial part of its flap volume to house additional fuel in addition to the main integral tanks in the inner wings.

First of the three P.1B prototypes, XA847, made its initial flight at Warton on 4 April 1957, once more in the hands of Beamont. The P.1B slipped easily through the transonic region to Mach 1.2 on this first flight, and it created another notable mark on 25 November 1958 by becoming the first British aircraft to reach Mach 2.0, which it did in level flight. It maintained that speed at the minimum afterburning setting, carrying a ventral tank, missile pylons and heavy instrumentation. With the good low-speed characteristics of its near-delta wings, which enabled it to be flown down to something like 100 knots (185 km/hr), the P.1B demonstrated the remarkable speed range of 13:1. After some 40 flights, XA847 had shown no significant handling problems, and the way was clear to go ahead with the precise measurement of its performance.

The three aerodynamic prototypes, XA847, XA853 and XA856, were allocated for engine, weapon and structural testing, but for the intensive proving of the various systems, the Ministry adopted the long-overdue course of ordering twenty more pre-production prototypes well before the first P.1Bs had flown. Such a quantity was considered adequate for the immediate programme of research and development facing the company. USAF programmes have been financed in an even more grandiose and determined manner; development test flying of the Convair F-102 was undertaken by 52 aircraft, together with two TF-102 two-seaters, and at any given time several F-102s were employed on drag measurements alone. Britain was the poor relation and could not afford to operate on such a scale. The twenty extra P.1 development aircraft were the most Britain could deploy to solve the technical problems ahead. Work began on the twenty development batch (DB) aircraft (XG307-313 and XG325-337) and the first of these flew initially on 3 April 1958.

Apart from equipment, there were no major differences from the first P.1Bs, although after the first three DB aircraft had been built, the original small fin and rudder was replaced by one of increased height and 30 per cent more area, to compensate for the destabilizing effect of the Firestreak (originally called Blue Jay) air-to-air missiles carried externally on the sides of the fuselage. All twenty DB aircraft were flying by the end of 1959, each allocated specific tasks in the development programme, covering such items as aerodynamics, armament, powerplants, electrics, autostabilization and so on, and many experiments were carried out under sortie conditions. XG307 to 310 all had split trailing edge flaps and did not have fuel in the flaps or leading edge.

Additional fuel capacity was introduced about half-way through the DB production programme, and after much speculation the new model was called 'Lightning' as from October 1958, although at one time 'Excalibur' had been favoured. Three of the last DBs, XG334, 335 and 336, were after preliminary completion of the tests, assigned in December 1959 to the Air Fighting Development Squadron (AFDS) at RAF Coltishall, Norfolk. There they were given the identity letters A, B and C and were subsequently used for flying experiments under operational conditions to sort out any snags, in the course of which XG334/'A' was lost because of hydraulic failure while flying off the Norfolk coast and crash-landed near Wells-next-the-Sea. A few weeks later, during an air-defence-exercise, the AFDS Lightning, flying from Leconfield in Yorkshire, attained a satisfactory interception rate and received rave reviews.

Associated development included installation of the Airpass radar system in a trials Dakota and a Canberra B.8, plus air-testing by de Havilland Propellers with the Firestreak AAM.

Two Firestreak heat-seeking missiles with

infrared heads were provided as primary armament for the P.1B, supplemented by two 30 mm Aden Mk 4 cannon mounted above the fuselage, where their pressure waves could not interfere with the intake flow. Additional punch was provided by two alternative installations in the lower fuselage, comprising either a further pair of Aden cannon in a quickly removable pack, or two retractable boxes containing 48 2 inch (50 mm) aircraft rockets. With either installation, re-arming and refuelling could be completed in less than ten minutes, while the weapon packs can be interchanged within an hour. Although some provision was made for other stores on the Lightning it was originally optimized for the point-defence interception role.

Structurally, the Lightning is completely conventional, built up of high-strength light alloys, titanium panels and metal-honeycomb sandwich

Beamont formates with the Meteor chase aircraft in P.1B XA847, now featuring a ventral fuel tank with stabilizing fin. The dorsal fin is reduced in area (BAe)

sections for the control surface extremities. The controls themselves are fully powered by duplicated hydraulic systems driven independently from each engine, and provided with spring feel, plus feel on the tailplane and rudder.

In November 1956 the RAF placed an order for an initial batch of Lightning F.1s. On 30 October 1959 the first production Lightning F.1, XM134, was rolled out for its first flight at Samlesbury and on 30 July 1960, fully combat-equipped Lightnings entered squadron service with No 74 Sqn.

No 74 Sqn was the first RAF front-line squadron to receive the Lightning. On 29 June 1960, XM165 (No 5, 'F') was taken on strength—the first Lightning delivered to the squadron. Serviceability reached nightmare proportions as the unit was working-up
(Flight)

TOP LEFT
The second P.1B, XA853, carrying two dummy Firestreak AAMs. XA853 was used for weapons system trials and a pre-production Ferranti Airpass AI.23 radar was installed. This view shows the straight leading edge to wing (note 'saw-cuts'), and the ventral tank
(BAe)

OPPOSITE
Target facilities Lightning F.1 XM164 in the twilight of its career at RAF Leuchars next to a Phantom FG.1 in about 1970. XM164 is also illustrated on this page (No 3, 'K') flying with No 74 Sqn

*Lightning F.1
cockpit: the radar
display (minus
rubber cover) is
visible below the
standby compass,
top right. The two
most important
instruments are
the fuel gauges,
bottom right
(BAe)*

The first Lightning F.2 XN723 during a test-sortie from Warton in late 1961. This aircraft crashed at Keyham, near Leicester, on 25 March 1964 (BAe)

TOP LEFT
Lightning F.1 XG331 was one of the 20 DB aircraft. This machine took part in tropical trials at Khormaksar at the end of 1961. The aircraft has a black spine and orange day-glo panels on the fin and forward fuselage (Flight)

OPPOSITE
The first P.1B, XA847, equipped for in-flight refuelling trials. A wide-angle camera (blister below canopy) was used to record 'contacts' with the crude probe. XA847 also has an early mock-up of the big ventral tank

Lightning F.1

The first Lightning F.1 (XM134) made its maiden flight on 30 October 1959, and after the type was released to the Central Fighter Establishment (CFE) on 14 May 1960, it entered squadron service with No 74 Sqn at RAF Coltishall on 29 June in the same year.

The Lightning F.1 was the operational version of the P.1B and 55 aircraft were ordered by the RAF, but five machines were subsequently cancelled, and a further three became test airframes. Although in principle an 'all-weather' interceptor, the F.1 did not have this capability in practice. Its basic navigation system, poor endurance, and missiles that were relatively ineffective except in a tail-chasing engagement in a clear air mass, did not confer any certainty of downing a target and safely recovering to base on a squally night. To be fair, most fighters do not live up to the brochure 'all-weather' tag either. In the case of the Lightning, its ability to respond in bad weather largely depends on crosswind limits (though these would naturally be waived in wartime), and whether individual pilots are capable of 'in-weather' flying at night. The skill of the fighter controller is also critical to a successful intercept by a single-seat fighter in particular.

On the plus side, despite serviceability headaches, the RAF had a fighter that could probably outclimb any other aircraft in the world in 1960, and for many years afterwards. (Why the RAF never attempted any time-to-height records remains something of a mystery.)

Production switched to the F.1A from the twentieth machine onwards. The F.1 was pensioned off as late as November 1974, and was latterly operated in the target facilities role.

Lightning F.1A

The first F.1A (XM169) flew on 16 August 1960 and entered service with No 56 Sqn at RAF Wattisham in Suffolk on 14 December in the same year.

In common with the majority of Lightning marks, the F.1A had provision for 48 × 2 in rockets in a pair of Mircrocell-reinforced plastic, retractable launchers in the ventral weapons pack, but the idea of killing aircraft with air-to-air rockets soon became distinctly *passé*. The built-in armament of two 30 mm Mk 4 Aden cannon, plus two Firestreak AAMs, proved to be the most effective option. The rockets had little value—poor visibility from the cockpit and horrendous fuel consumption at low level made the Lightning unsuitable for any secondary ground attack role. (Years later, the Lightning F.2As of Nos 19 and 92 Sqns based at RAF Gütersloh in West Germany, had to be prepared to switch from air defence to ground strafing if the Red hordes poured over the border.) Two additional Aden cannon could be carried as an alternative to the rockets and missile pack. Ferranti Airpass AI.23 radar was fitted.

The power to win was produced by two Rolls-Royce Avon 210 (RA.24R) turbojets developing 14,430 lb (6,545 kg) of static thrust with afterburning. This engine also powered the P.1B, F.1, F.2 and T.4. Despite being a somewhat thirsty powerplant, the Avon was (and still is) a genuine 'fighter engine', and was especially tolerant of throttle-slamming at both high and low altitudes. The engine could take the use and abuse associated with rapid transitions from military power to reheat thrust settings in the heat of combat. Fuel was housed in integral wing and flap tanks, and a 250 Imp gal (1,136 lit) jettisonable ventral tank. A detachable in-flight refuelling probe could be fitted under the port wing.

Structurally, the Lightning was completely conventional. The wing was an all-metal, five-spar surface utilizing English Electric's ASN/P1/3 section sweptback 60° on the leading edge, 52° on the trailing edge, and a thickness/chord ratio of 5 per cent. This wing was common to the P.1A, P.1B, F.1, F.2, and T.4. 'Saw-cut' notches were incorporated in the leading edge. The wing was constructed by joining the two panels at the centreline, and the upper and lower skins were generally 0.2 in (0.5 cm) thick.

The fuselage and fin were similarly all-metal. All the control surfaces, and the airbrakes, were hydraulically operated. The rudder was made of metal honeycomb sandwich throughout, and the ailerons, all-moving tailplane, and the top of the fin had metal honeycomb sandwich tips.

The tricycle landing gear was jointly designed by English Electric and Messier. Maxaret anti-skid brakes were standard. The wheels were manufactured by Dunlop, and the tyres inflated to 280 lb/in² (19.3 kg/cm²). Even at this very high pressure, the main gear tyres were still too thick to

lie flush inside the wing and the gear doors had to be bulged. Main gear track measured 12 ft 9.3 in (3.89 m). Braking was assisted by a 16 ft (4.8 m) Irving ribbon parachute packed into the bottom of the rear fuselage.

Other equipment included a Martin-Baker Type 4BS ejection seat, Elliot autopilot (with attitude hold and ILS coupling), UHF, TACAN, and IFF. The F.1A was withdrawn in July 1974.

Lightning F.2

The first Lightning F.2 (XN723) flew on 11 July 1961, and after being released to the CFE on 14 November 1962, this variant entered service with No 19 Sqn at RAF Leconfield on 17 December in the same year.

The F.2 differed only in detail from the F.1A, introducing nose-wheel steering, improved reheat, a liquid oxygen breathing system, a standby turbo generator for the DC electric supply (cooled by a small scoop intake on the dorsal spine—an external recognition feature), and a revised cockpit (incorporating part of OR946) with a new basic 'T' of flight instruments including a 'roller-blind' horizon. Ferranti had offered the RAF a fully automatic, autonomous, interception system, similar in concept to the equipment installed in the Convair F-106 Delta Dart (see chapter 4), but it was cancelled. In general, the flight performance of the F.2 was superior to the F.1A, flying faster, higher and longer. Only 44 F.2s were built and 31 were converted into F.2As from 1966 (next entry). A few F.2s survive as airfield decoys, but this mark was officially retired in May 1974.

Lightning F.2A

The first F.2 (XN781) arrived at Warton for rebuilding into an F.2A on 13 September 1966 and it re-entered service with No 19 Sqn at RAF Gütersloh on 26 February 1968. The type served exclusively with Nos 19 and 92 Sqns in West Germany, and many pilots considered the F.2A the best of the breed. Its safety record was exemplary.

Two nose-mounted 30 mm Aden cannon were retained, the blast tubes being the most visible difference between this mark and the F.6. Most F.6 features were incorporated into the F.2A, including the cambered leading edge to the wing, larger ventral tank, cropped fin and arrestor hook, but not the overwing tanks (not really needed in air defence operations over Germany), or Red Top AAMs.

The F.2A was the last Lightning mark to be 'built' and it retired in April 1974. Many are currently used as airfield decoys.

Lightning F.3

The first F.3 DB machine (XG310) flew in November 1961, and the first production F.3 (XP693) made its maiden flight on 16 June 1962. XP695 was released to the CFE on 1 January 1964 and the F.3 entered service with No 74 Sqn at RAF Leuchars on 14 April in the same year (XP700). F.3s are still active with the LTF at Binbrook.

The F.3 introduced the Avon 301 series turbojet developing 16,360 lb (7,420 kg) of static thrust with reheat (which was fully variable, at last). Another major change was the deletion of gun armament (a short-sighted blunder), but the more advanced AI.23B radar and associated Red Top AAMs gave the Lightning a much-needed collision-course attack capability for the first time. The cockpit had the full OR946 navigation system with a Mk 2 MRG (master reference gyro). To maintain directional stability at high-Mach with the larger missiles, the fin was cropped at the tip and its area increased by 15 per cent. Further aerodynamic fine-tuning was applied to the wing, the tips being arrowed at a more acute angle. The Avon 301 and modified wing were common to the T.5. UHF homing aerials are positioned on the

Another view of F.2 XN734, this time landing back at Warton with brake parachute deployed and airbrakes cracked open
(BAe)

Beamont flying the prototype Lightning F.3 (a conversion of the DB machine XG310), which introduced the larger cropped fin, AI.23B radar and Red Top AAMs. The two 30 mm Aden cannons were deleted—a big mistake. XG310 first flew in F.3 guise on 18 November 1961 (BAe)

fuselage behind the canopy. VHF/UHF aerials are situated on the fin tip and under the nose.

The last F.3 (XR720) was delivered to No 56 Sqn on 8 April 1965. Some late production aircraft were converted to interim F.6 standard.

Lightning F.6

The first flight of an interim F.6 (XP697) occurred on 17 April 1964. The first production F.6 (XR752, interim version) flew on 16 June 1965. During 1967–68 interim F.6s were cycled through Warton for modification to full F.6 standard by BAC. Released to the CFE on 16 November 1965 (XR753), the F.6 entered front-line service with No 5 Sqn when XR755 and XR756 were delivered to RAF Binbrook on 10 December 1965. The first full production F.6 was XR768. This variant is currently in service with Nos 5 and 11 Sqns and the LTF at RAF Binbrook.

The Lightning F.6 is an enhanced derivative of

the F.3 and has the same weapons system. Guns returned to the Lightning when the type was modified to full F.6 standard. Both guns were fitted in the front section of the enlarged ventral tank, which has a total capacity of 610 Imp gal (2,773 lit), and 535 Imp gal (2,432 lit) when the guns are installed. The bigger ventral tank causes less drag, but splayed fins were needed on the underside to maintain directional stability at high-Mach. Additional fuel could be carried in overwing tanks (a unique feature), each capable of holding 260 Imp gal (1,181 lit) of fuel. Total fuel capacity using all tanks is 1,846 Imp gal (8,390 lit). The F.3 can also carry overwing tanks. The

installation was test-flown on the third F.2, XN725. The F.6 is powered by Avon 302 series turbojets producing 16,300 lb (7,393 kg) of static thrust with reheat. Thanks to its raw thrust reserve and consistent handling, further improved by the cambered leading edge of the wing, the Lightning can successfully 'mix-it' with more modern fighters such as the Mirage F.1, and can give an F-4 a very hard time indeed. However, in common with many fellow fighter drivers, Lightning pilots have a great respect for the F-15 Eagle and F-16 Falcon.

Lightning F.53

The ultimate development of the Lightning, the F.53 is the 'multi-role' version of the F.6 ordered by Saudi Arabia and Kuwait. The first F.53 (53–666) made its maiden flight on 1 November 1966, and the first example (53-667) was delivered to the Royal Saudi Air Force on 4 December 1967. Kuwait's F.53s have since been replaced by

A bastard—Lightning F.2 XN734 was used as a development aircraft for the F.3 programme and test-flew the Avon 301 engine, fueldraulic system, and overwing + ventral tank/cropped fin/Red Top configuration (BAe)

Mirage F.1s, but Lightnings remain operational with No 2 Sqn RSAF at Dhahran pending the arrival of F-15s.

Many pundits predicted that the 'plumber's nightmare of an aeroplane' would not adapt well to the desert environment. They were right. The baking heat and mischievous sand brought serviceability levels to an all-time low on some occasions. The offer of lucrative contracts to fly F.53s persuaded many RAF pilots to move to the Middle East. Their presence was vital until a cadre of experienced Arab pilots could be trained to fly Lightnings. Pakistani personnel are also much in evidence in the RSAF today. The Lightning has played a key role in bringing Saudi

27

The variable-camber wing of the Lightning F.6 is shown to advantage in this view of XR754, an interim version without Aden cannons in the enlarged ventral tank. Note the splayed ventral fins
(BAe)

OPPOSITE PAGE
Lightning F.6 cockpit with the ejector seat removed. Compare with the F.1 cockpit on pages 20–21. The main panel on the F.6 is revised and simplified. A strip-speed indicator is located below the gunsight

Arabia and Kuwait into contact with sophisticated Western defence technology, and the stability of the Gulf may well depend on how well they can operate it.

The F.53 is powered by Avon 302-C turbojets producing 16,300 lb (7,393 kg) of static thrust with reheat. Armament details can be found in chapter 5. See also Lightnings for export at the end of this chapter. Other equipment specified for the F.53 included the Martin-Baker Type BS4 C Mk 2 ejection seat (effective down to 90 knots (167 km/h) at zero altitude), and Ferranti AI.23S radar. Additional avionics were also fitted.

Saudi Lightnings were supported by the invaluable assistance of the British Aircraft Corporation, and purpose-built facilities were installed for training, maintenance, and operations. The introduction of the Lightning put Saudi Arabia into a position which gave them technical parity with their more strident Arab neighbours, especially Syria and Egypt, though the latter subsequently became more moderate in outlook.

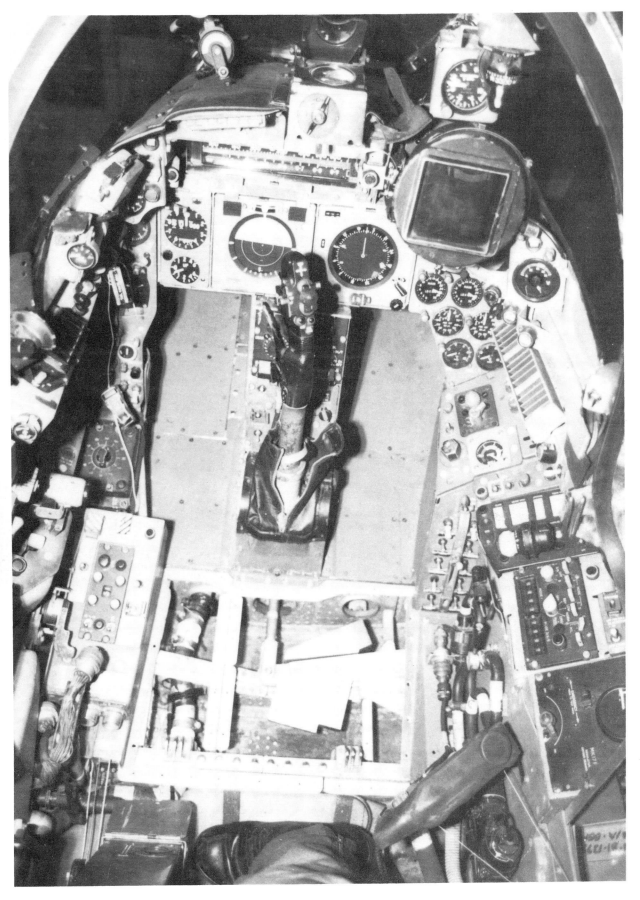

Two-Seat Trainers

Three versions of the BAC Lightning trainer were
built; the T.4, T.5 and T.55. During the model
testing of the Lightning prototypes the Ministry of
Supply ordered the development of a two-seater
intended for training as well as operational roles.
For pilot conversion it is both quicker and safer
with a two-seat version of an operational aircraft.
The two-seat Lightning was originally known as
the English Electric P.11 and English Electric
derived it from an F.1A. The type was
subsequently designated T.4.

To accommodate the two side-by-side Martin-
Baker Mk 4BS ejector seats the front of the
fuselage in the area of the cockpit was widened on
both sides and the front fuselage was 11.5 inch (29
cm) wider than the single-seat version. The front
fuselage was bulbous, but the rear was identical to
the F.1A. Not only were the flying controls
duplicated, but also the Airpass radar displays.
The T.4 was powered by two Rolls-Royce Avon
210 turbojets with four stages of reheat. The
armament was as the F.1, but the 30 mm Aden
guns were no longer fixed and could be carried in
the ventral pack. The T.4 was a two-seat dual
control side-by-side operational trainer for F.1,
F.1A, F.2 and F.2A. Since the performance and
equipment of the trainer version is virtually
identical to the single-seat Lightnings, they can be
used for operational duties.

The first prototype (XL628) flew at Warton
with 'Roly' Beamont at the controls on 6 May
1959. On 1 October 1959, John Squier, chief
experimental test pilot for English Electric,
climbed into the cockpit of XL628 for another test
sortie. He was briefed for a full aileron roll at
Mach 1.7 at 40,000 ft (12,192 m) with Firestreaks
fitted. XL628 started the manoeuvre and as Squier
centralized the controls to stop the roll, the aircraft
yawed violently and the fin broke with a loud
bang. The aircraft immediately went out of control
and as the pilot felt himself losing consciousness
he reached up and pulled the face blind, which
operated the ejector seat. After $28\frac{1}{4}$ hours in the
water John Squier landed in Wigtown Bay in
western Scotland, cold and wet.

The first production Lightning T.4, XM966,
made its first flight on 15 July 1960. The original
order for thirty aircraft was later cut to twenty and
the first of these, XM970, entered RAF service
with the Lightning Conversion Squadron (LCS) at
Middleton St George on 29 June 1962. The LCS

*The prototype Lightning T.4 trainer XL628 being flown by
Beamont over Warton in 1958. Another company test
pilot, John Squier, was forced to eject from this aircraft on
1 October 1959. It crashed into the Irish Sea
(BAe)*

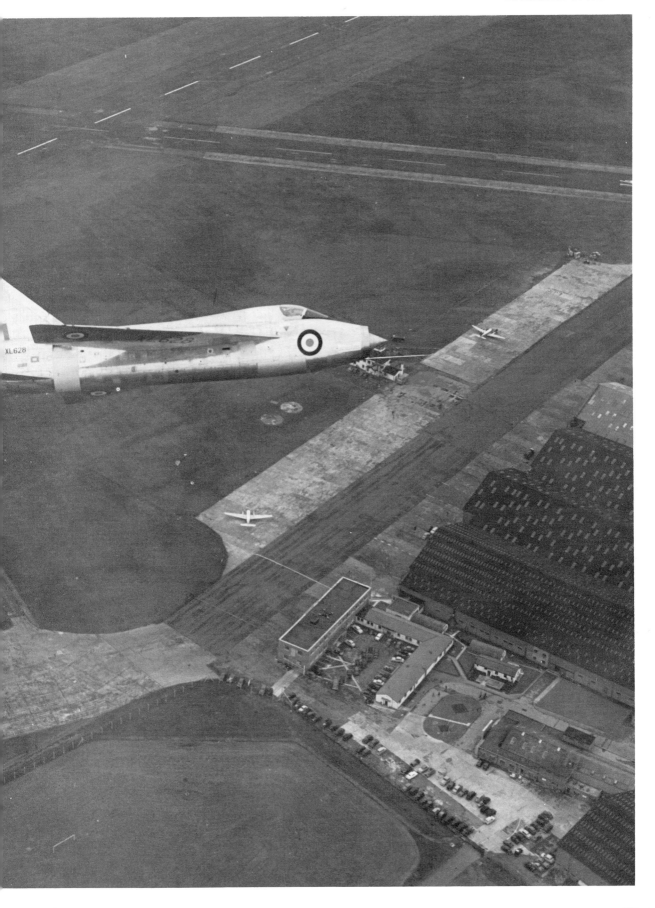

Lightning T.5 cockpit which features duplicated radar displays fitted with rubber covers—the symbology on the screen is difficult to read without them. This 'head-down' display is a major handicap in air combat. Only one gunsight is fitted (left), and the ejection seats have been removed

TOP LEFT
Another shot of T.4 XL628 at Farnborough in 1958, resplendent with black spine and orange day-glo panels on nose and fin, but retaining its yellow day-glo RAF Training Command band on the rear fuselage. Dummy Firestreaks are fitted
(Flight)

OPPOSITE
Factory-fresh Lightning T.4s wait in wintry conditions at Warton prior to delivery to the LCS at RAF Middleton St George in the early 1960s. The nearest T.4, XM993, overshot the runway at Middleton St George on 12 December 1962 and burnt out
(BAe)

received ten aircraft which were exclusively used for the retraining of pilots. Apart from the LCS a T.4 was also issued to each Lightning squadron and the AFDS for routine training during 1962 to 1964. XM988 went to No 19 Sqn, XM989 to No 56, XM992 to No 111, XM995 to No 92 and No 74 was loaned XM974 from the AFDS. XM974 was subsequently taken on charge by No 74 Sqn, and carried the tailcode letter 'T'.

Some T.4s, redesignated T.54, were supplied to the Royal Saudi Air Force as interim trainers in 1966 (see Lightnings for Export).

The Lightning T.5 was derived from the F.3. The prototype, XM967, was produced at the beginning of 1962 as a modification of a T.4 and on 29 March 1962 with 'Jimmy' Dell at the controls it flew at Filton for the first time. The T.5 is as the F.3, the rear fuselage identical to the

Two pilots wearing full pressure suits about to make their exit left from a Lightning T.4. Unusually, this aircraft is fitted with two Aden cannons in the ventral weapons pack (BAe)

OPPOSITE
The prototype Lightning T.5 XM967 which first flew on 30 March 1962. Cropped fin and Red Top armament are distinguishing marks. This aircraft was sent to the fire dump at RAF Kemble in 1976 after flying less than 500 hours (BAe)

F.3, but the front fuselage bulbous. Externally different from T.4 by squared topped fin and longer cable ducting. Same armament as F.3 and it can be used in the air interception role armed with Red Tops. Operational trainer for the F.3 and F.6.

The first production Lightning T.5, XS417 flew on 17 July, 1964. As follow on unit of the LCS, No 226 OCU at RAF Coltishall took delivery of the first T.5, XS419, on 20 April 1965.

As replacements for XS453, which crashed on 1 July 1966, and XS460, transferred to Saudi Arabia and crashed at Warton 7 March 1967, two further T.5 aircraft XV328 and XV329 were built after the mark had been out of production for almost a year. XV328 flew on December 22nd, 1966 and then delivered to 60MU before transferring to No 29 Sqn at Wattisham. XV329 flew on December 30th and on 8 March 1967 was delivered to Sydenham, Belfast for shipment to Tengah for No 74 Sqn.

A total of 22 T.5 machines were built and many of them are still flying at Binbrook.

The T.55, with the modified wings and extra fuel capacity of the F.53, was the export version of the T.5. This two-seat operational trainer for the F.53 multi-role fighter, with the same interceptor armament as the F.53, was ordered by Saudi Arabia and Kuwait. (see Lightnings for Export). The first T.55 (55-710) flew on 3 November 1966. First delivery to Royal Saudi Air Force (55-711) on 18 December 1967.

Lightnings for Export

The more realistic endurance of the Lightning F.6 made the aircraft a better proposition for the export market. Finally, the exportable F.53 transformed the Lightning from an interceptor into an aircraft that could be quickly adapted to attack, reconnaissance or interception duties; or a combination of all three. However, despite strenuous sales efforts in South America, the Far and Middle East, and Europe, little interest was shown. The Lightning was expensive to buy and costly to operate. Therefore, it was an uphill battle and the Lightning was a disaster in the export market. The Lockheed F-104 and Dassault Mirage had already carved up the world market for supersonic fighters by the mid-1960s.

After a hard sales drive Saudi Arabia showed interest and in December 1965 it was announced that Britain had won a £100 million defence contract with Saudi Arabia, comprising Lightning fighters, Strikemaster training aircraft, AEI radar, communications and data-handling equipment (worth £25 million) and Airwork support and training facilities valued at £20 million.

The Royal Saudi Air Force had an offensive element of nine F-86F Sabres and an attack force of a similar number of B-26 Invaders. As such, the RSAF was incapable of preventing air raids and intrusions by hostile aircraft.

Thirty-four of a new Lightning mark, the F.53 (multi-role version of F.6), were required plus six T.55 trainers, (export version of T.5). They were serialled 53-666 to 53-700 and 55-711 to 55-716 respectively. A year after the first F.53 flew in November 1966, the first aircraft was delivered to the RSAF.

To fill the gap before delivery of the order began, the RAF agreed to release four F.2s, XN767, 770, 796 and 797, from storage at No 33 MU, and two T.4s XM989 (ex-No 56 Sqn) and XM992 (ex-226 OCU), recently replaced by new T.5s. These were sold to the RSAF and after modification at Warton, the six flew to Dhahran where Airwork personnel were waiting for them. Designated F.52 and T.54 respectively, they entered service serialled 52-655 to 52-658 and 54-

650 and 54-651. As the RAF could spare no more trainers, the Saudis also acquired two Hunter T.7s, XL620, converted to Mark 70 serial, 70-616, and XL605 converted to Mark 70, serial 70-617, and these were used to train RSAF pilots as a lead-in to the Lightning conversion programme.

The Lightnings formed the initial equipment of No 6 Sqn and were used for training at Khamis Mushayt in Saudi Arabia until the arrival of the F.53s and T.55s.

Following the crash of an F.52 at Riyadh on 22 September 1966, a fifth F.2, XN729, was prepared by BAC, using for the first time the company Class-B civil marking 'G27' (without hyphen). G27-1 was delivered as 52-629 and later became '612' before it too crashed, on 2 May 1970.

The prototype of the F.53 was XR722 and its first flight as an F.3 was on 23 January 1965. It was converted to first F.53 and flew again on 19 October 1966 as G27-2, Saudi serial 53-666. After remaining at Warton as a test aircraft, it left as G27-37-1G on 28 August 1969, and served with No 1 Sqn until it crashed at Khamis Mushayt on 6 February 1972.

G27-37/53-667 was the first new Saudi aircraft and the last, G27-69/53-699 was delivered on 4 June 1968. The aircraft were delivered by British pilots, who had a contract to train both air and groundcrews. A similar production procedure was followed with the T.55s and the prototype was XS460, which first flew on 31 January 1966 as 55-710. It was damaged beyond repair when it ran off the runway at Warton on 7 March 1967 and the replacement G27-70/55-711 was not available until September. The T.55s were originally delivered to No 226 OCU at Coltishall in February 1968 to train Saudi pilots, before forming their own OCU at Dhahran.

Border disputes brought the Lightnings to war and they fired their first shots in anger when they were used for ground strafing against rebels. During one such sortie in May 1970, 53-697 was reported to have crashed inside the Yemen.

The Lightnings are being replaced by 62 McDonnell Douglas F-15 Eagles.

The only other country to purchase Lightnings

TOP
The first Lightning F.53 carrying two 1,000 lb (454 kg) bombs and wearing the Class-B registration G-27-2. Converted from an F.3 (XR722), this aircraft later became 53-666 with the Royal Saudi Air Force. It crashed into the Gulf on 6 February 1972 (BAe)

Lightning F.53 armed with 4 × Matra 155 launchers housing eighteen 68 mm SNEB rockets, and 48 × 2 inch spin-stabilized rockets in retractable launchers under the forward fuselage, the latter one of a number of weapon pack options including five Vinten Type 360 70 mm cameras

was Kuwait; 12 F.53s, serial 53-412–53-423 and two T.55s, serial 55-410 and 55-411, were delivered during 1968–69 and based at Kuwait airport. The training of the Kuwaiti pilots was also undertaken by No 226 OCU.

However, the Lightning was not successful in Kuwait and proved too complex a machine for the desert environment. After seven years the Lightning fleet was grounded. The Lightnings were replaced from 1977 by 30 Mirage F.1s.

Three factories with a total workforce of 8,000 were involved in the production of the Lightning. Wings and fuselages were made at the English Electric Preston works; the main fuselage and tail surfaces at Accrington; and the final assembly line at the English Electric Samlesbury factory. The completed aircraft made their initial flight from the aerodrome at Samlesbury and flown straight to the company's main aerodrome at Warton, where all test flying was done. A few conversions (e.g. F.2 to F.2A), were done at Wolverhampton by Boulton and Paul; the nearest airfield was Seighford near Stafford. Production and delivery of RAF Lightning variants was completed in 1967.

Good Points of the Lightning

From the pilot's point of view the cockpit is quite sound and considering the age of the aircraft the cockpit is well laid out. However, in the light of more modern developments a pilot can see a lot of limitations in it. Inside missile range the pilot has to select guns. In order to do that the pilot has to change hands—normally right hand on stick—in order to reach down with his right hand to the starboard console to operate Master Armament Select (MAS) to guns. HOTAS (hands-on-the-throttle-and-stick) operation would be a godsend for a Lightning jockey. The strip speed in the Lightning is clear and easy to read.
—Quick reaction aircraft from 2 minutes readiness—i.e. the pilot in the cockpit, very easy to make that time.
—Fantastic airframe performance for its generation.
—Good on climb, always lots of power and high rate of roll. Can also roll and pull-it. In the Voodoo, the pilot had to ease off the back pressure, roll the aircraft in the direction he wanted to go, then re-apply the back pressure and start pulling again.

Line-up of Lightning F.53s at Warton prior to delivery to the Royal Saudi Air Force in 1967 (BAe)

One of 12 Lightning F.53s purchased by Kuwait. G27-80 became 53-412
(BAe)

TOP LEFT
One of the RAF T.4s (XM989) transferred to the Royal Saudi Air Force as 54-650. The roundel appears on the rear fuselage—rather unusual. This aircraft was subsequently re-numbered 54-607
(BAe)

OPPOSITE
Lightning F.6 XR770 wearing spurious Saudi markings (the number 53-770 appears in Arabic on fin), at the 1966 Farnborough Air Show—a year after BAC's sales coup in the Middle East. Dummy Firestreaks fitted for effect
(BAe)

—The Lightning at high level is good and will fly comfortably subsonic and supersonic, and is a delight to fly up to its service ceiling. Because of the oxygen system and the pilot's personal equipment the single-seat Lightning F.3 and F.6 are limited to 50,000 ft (15,240 m) and the T.5 to 43,000 ft (13,106 m) (this has a different oxygen regulator). Otherwise the Lightning is cleared to 60,000 ft (18,288 m). However, many pilots have been above that height, mostly on airtest. One pilot claims to have been to 78,000 ft (23,780 m). At that height the aircraft is virtually ballistic.

—The engine arrangement is good with one engine being above the other. Very easy to fly on one engine (no assymmetric problem). No critical areas while on one engine, except with overwing fuel tanks just after take-off. Also, because of only one intake, no intake drag if one engine shut down.

—The only aircraft in the world with overwing fuel tanks. They produce a fair amount of drag, but 2,000 lb (908 kg) of fuel in each. Operationally, overwing tanks are a drawback because they impose an airspeed limit—525 knots or Mach .98. Can only pull a maximum

*Lead aircraft is a Lightning T.55 trainer bought by
Kuwait (G27-78, 55-410/'A'), flanked by Saudi F.53
G27-56 (nearest), and RAF Lightning F.6 XR759
(BAe)*

Lightning T.55 trainers of the Royal Saudi Air Force (BAe)

4G with the tanks on. They are therefore only ferry tanks.

All pilots agree that the Lightning is a beautiful aeroplane to fly and it will glide for miles.

Bad Points of the Lightning

The list is long, but the Lightning is very much a pilot's aircraft.

—The visibility from the cockpit is not very good and to look behind is very difficult—the Lightning needs a bubble canopy like the F-15 or F-16.

The crosswind limit on the Lightning is respected by all the pilots. By virtue of its design, engines on top of one another and the large fin to keep it straight at Mach 2.2, it has a large side area.

High landing speed at 175 mph/(281 km/h).

Therefore needs 7,500 ft (2,286 m) runway for normal operation. With a high landing speed also uses tyres very quickly. In crosswind (i.e. 20–25 knots/37–46 km/h) can use one set of tyres in one take-off and landing.

Normal operation on landing requires brake parachute to slow down the aircraft—landing roll increased and brake wear increased without brake 'chute.

Fuel consumption with Avon engine high, therefore 'short legs' for transit and patrol sorties. The average sortie length for the F.6 is 1 hour, the F.3 and T.5 only 40 minutes. On the F.6 this is extended with overwing fuel tanks to 1 hour 30 minutes, but as previously stated there are

Four Lightning F.53s (nearest) and two T.55 trainers at the end of the Warton production line and destined for Saudi Arabia
(BAe)

penalties.

Weapons system—very limited—only two missiles and two guns. The guns carry only 120 rounds each. Very basic gunsight, which is just a series of rings and very difficult to operate. It is set for range, airspeed and angle of attack. As one pilot put it: 'A bloody awful gunsight'.

Servicing—it is a plumber's nightmare of an aeroplane. Much of the system is very inaccessible and many parts have to be removed to get at the one that is faulty. The Avpin starter system is difficult to operate (volatile liquid) and easily contaminated by water in bad weather.

Start/turnround requires large ground-based power sets.

Ejection seat limited use: ground level at 90 knots.

Avionics limited—Tacan, ILS, VHF/UHF radio, compass and little else. IFF/SSR. Autopilot limited use. Radar limited capability.

Does not have Infrared Sighting & Tracking System (IRSTS) which allows the pilot to lock on to infrared emissions from a target aircraft. This can be very useful in a jamming environment.

Lightning now an old aircraft and fatigue is closely monitored.

Chapter 2
Lightning Squadrons

No 5 Sqn

Motto: *Frangas non flectas* (Thou mayest break but shall not bend)

No 5 Sqn was one of the original units of the Royal Flying Corps and among many other distinctions in its long history, No 5 Sqn was the first squadron to be issued with the F.6 version of the Lightning. It will also lay claim to being the longest operator of the Lightning.

After a spell with Vampire FB.5s and Meteor NF.11s, No 5 Sqn began to re-equip with Javelin FAW.5s in February, 1960. In November 1962 the squadron moved to Geilenkirchen and re-equipped with Javelin FAW.9s. On 7 October 1965, the squadron disbanded at Geilenkirchen and re-formed the following day at RAF Binbrook, Lincolnshire, under the command of Wg Cdr L J Hargreaves.

Until the arrival of a T.5 (XS451) on 19 November the squadron had to make do with a Hunter T.7A (WV318) which had been specially modified to incorporate the special OR946 instrumentation of the Lightning F.3 and F.6 and was to serve as a systems trainer until the T-birds arrived. The first 'interim' F.6s, XR755/'A' and XR756/'B' arrived on 10 December 1965.

Over the next few weeks the Lightnings arrived in small numbers and the squadron did not receive its twelfth aircraft (XR765) until 8 March 1966. Because of the slow delivery rate the squadron did not become fully operational until well into the

OPPOSITE PAGE
Eleven Lightning F.6s of No 5 Sqn (the 'Fighting Fifth') form their squadron number over Binbrook in April 1970. Only five aircraft have in-flight refuelling probes (Crown copyright)

Lightning F.6 (XS894/'F') of No 5 Sqn armed with live Red Tops makes a fast getaway from RAF Binbrook in April 1970. XS894 crashed off Flamborough Head on September 9th in the same year (Crown copyright)

*Lightning F.1A (XM183/'X') of No 5 Sqn in use as a
target facilities aircraft at Binbrook in the early 1970s*

TOP
*Lightning F.6 (XS895/'B') of No 5 Sqn taxies back to the
flight line after a sortie from Binbrook in 1972*

year. The aircraft were marked with red rectangles astride the roundel and a green maple leaf in a white disc on the fin.

No 74 Sqn was the first squadron to receive the F.6, and after the 'Tigers' were fully equipped, XS894/'F' was delivered to No 5 Sqn on 3 January 1967 to start the replacement of the interim F.6s, all of which went back to Warton for conversion to full F.6 standard along with some of the stored F.3s.

Having traded-in its interim F.6s for the full F.6 standard in the spring of 1967, the squadron participated in ADEX 67, and was based at Luqa

Lightning F.6 (XS926/'B') of No 5 Sqn starts its take-off roll. A Maltese Cross is carried on the fin—evidence of a recent deployment to RAF Luqa. This aircraft was lost on 22 September 1969
(Grimsby Evening Telegraph)

OVERLEAF
Flt Lt Al Davey on the grass at Binbrook with his Lightning F.6 in May 1967. (See same Lightning on page 47). Davey casually parked his flying helmet on the port Firestreak. Note makeshift ladder and raised barrier
(Crown copyright)

Lightning F.6 (XS901/'D') of No 5 Sqn taking-off from Binbrook in the late 1960s. This aircraft currently serves with No 11 Sqn as 'BH'

OPPOSITE
A vic of Lightning F.6s (interim versions) of No 5 Sqn photographed in 1969. The two black Firestreak missiles are drill rounds—the rest are live. At the time of writing all three aircraft (XR760/'F' (see page 56), XR758/'D', and XR754/'G') are still in service (Crown copyright)

in Malta between 6 and 26 October. When the Lightnings arrived back at Binbrook they carried a day-glo Maltese Cross marking on the fin.

In May 1968, four Lightnings from No 5 Sqn flew non-stop from Binbrook to Bahrain, covering 4,000 miles (6,437 km) in eight hours, refuelled en route by Victors from RAF Marham. That same year the squadron won the Dacre Trophy, which is awarded for weapons proficiency to the top UK fighter squadron. At the Farnborough Air Show in September the squadron put up two Lightnings for a flight refuelling demonstration. In July 1969 six Lightnings took part in the flypast during the Investiture of Prince Charles at Caernarvon. That same year the squadron again won the Dacre Trophy. In December 1969, ten Lightnings of No 5 Sqn went to RAF Tengah on the eastern side of Singapore for joint air-defence exercises with other RAF Lightning units and RAAF Mirages, to demonstrate Strike Command's ability to reinforce Far East bases.

1970 saw the squadron deployed to Singapore, where it took part in local defence exercises. Replacement Lightnings were ferried to No 74 Sqn, and No 5 Sqn returned with some 74 Sqn Lightnings which were due for major overhaul in the UK.

Wg Cdr D R Kuun made a successful belly landing in Lightning F.6 (XR752/'H') of No 5 Sqn. The aircraft sustained category 2 damage which cost £99,000 to fix. A wheels-up landing is a risky option—if a wing touches the ground the aircraft is likely to cartwheel

TOP RIGHT
The last photograph of Lightning F.6 XR765. Flt Lt 'Jim' Wild taxies out in camouflaged 'AJ' of No 5 Sqn—a mere 30 minutes from an early bath. A reheat fire obliged Wild to abandon the aircraft off Flamborough Head just after 09.00 Zulu on 23 July 1981. (See page 167)

OPPOSITE
Lightning F.3 (XR718/'AS') of No 5 Sqn lets it all hang out. Ex-LTF aircraft with code letter 'C' still showing on fin

TOP
Lightning F.6s of No 5 Sqn on finals into Binbrook, 7 March 1977. Nearest aircraft (XR760/'G') with white code letter

Lightning F.3 (XP751/'AQ') landing at Binbrook, March 1983

TOP
Lightning F.6 (XS928/'K') taxies out at Binbrook, 9 February 1977

Unique Lightning F.6 (XS898/'J') of No 5 Sqn in experimental markings—green maple leaf on red bar and red code letter on fin

*Two-tone Barley grey F.6, with oversize 'pink and lilac'
national markings*

OPPOSITE
*Lightning F.6 (XR773/'AF') of No 5 Sqn piloted by Flt
Lt M R Tuffs overflying RAF Akrotiri, Cyprus in 1983.
The runway is visible at right of picture*

In the early 1970s the squadron identified itself
by encircling the maple leaf on the fin with a large
red '5'.

In 1970 and 1971, No 5 Sqn won the
Huddleston Trophy as the best NATO interceptor
squadron in the Allied Forces Central Europe
Annual Air Defence Competition. The Lightnings
defeated Phantoms, Starfighters and Mirages and
brought home the trophy to the United Kingdom.

During the next decade No 5 Sqn operated
alongside the other Binbrook Lightnings. Then a
change was in the wind. But not for the
Lightnings—it was the turn of the squadron's old
silk and gold standard bearing battle honours from
World War I right through to the Burma
Campaign of 1944 and 1945 which after 25 years'
was rather moth-eaten.

On 11 August 1983, Air Vice Marshal G A
White, who, 11 years previously, was No 5 Sqn's
commander, made the presentation and two flights
of No 5 Sqn paraded to the accompaniment of the
Royal Air Force College Band from Cranwell. The
standard was blessed by the Chaplain-in-Chief of
the RAF, the Ven G R Renowden. While the new
banner will take pride of place with No 5 Sqn's
other treasures, the old one will hang permanently
in the church of St Mary and St Gabriel,
Binbrook. A special service to lay-up the standard
was held in the church on Sunday 14 August
1983.

No 11 Sqn
Motto: *Ociores acrioresque aquilis* (Swifter and keener than eagles)

To fill the air defence gap No 11 Sqn was re-formed on Lightnings in April 1967. This was the first time the squadron had been in the UK since the 1920s. From 1 February 1929 until it re-formed at Leuchars the squadron had served in India, Singapore, Aden, Greece, Iraq, Egypt, Burma, Malaya, Japan and Germany. Since 1972 'The Eagles' have been based at Binbrook with No 5 Sqn and only the latter unit has operated the Lightning for a longer period.

With the conversion in December 1962 to Javelin FAW.9s, No 11 Sqn entered the modern era of fighters. It now carried Firestreak air-to-air missiles in addition to the guns. To fit them for high-altitude operations, crews wore pressure jerkins and had special training in aviation medicine.

The Javelin had been prone to spinning problems. With its high tailplane, it was apt to enter a very deep stall and the elevators then became ineffective. Fortunately this had not resulted in any fatalities on No 11 Sqn, although one pilot returned home without his navigator who had ejected during the spin. By 1965, however, fatigue cracks, frequently formed around the fin, made it all too apparent that the Javelin's days were numbered. For the third time in its history, No 11 Sqn was disbanded, on 12 January 1966.

On 1 April 1967, No 11 Sqn re-formed at Leuchars in Scotland, to become the third squadron flying Lightning F.6s equipped with Red Top air-to-air missiles. No 11 Sqn had re-formed to take over the air defence task from No 74 Sqn which was moving to Singapore. The squadron's first aircraft was XS904, and by mid-June they were up to strength on late production F.6s. The squadron had officially taken over its duties on May 15, alongside its partner in the Leuchars Lightning Wing, No 23 Sqn. As an all-weather single-seat fighter, the Lightning's task was standard peacetime training and regular periods of Battle Flight readiness. The latter was now known as either Interceptor Alert Force (IAF) or Quick Reaction Alert (QRA). Because of their geographical position, the squadron crews were regularly called to intercept Russian aircraft and during one day in April 1970, a total of forty identifications were made—twenty *Bears* and twenty *Badgers*. Sometimes, however, the pilots escorted airliners and light aircraft.

The new role of overseas reinforcement had been added and the squadron began regular air-to-air refuelling practice with both Victor and KC-135 tankers. On 29 November 1967, Flt Lt Eggleton set a record of 8¼ hours' flying; he refuelled five times and flew a total of 5,000 miles

No 11 Sqn received its fair share of Lightning F.3s. XR720/'M' served with the LTF as 'DA'

BELOW
Lightning F.6 (XS929/'E') of No 11 Sqn about to hit the concrete at Binbrook in March 1972. Note the overwing tanks
(Crown copyright)

OPPOSITE
Lightning F.6 (XR763/'B') at RAF Leuchars in February 1971. This interim version has a small fin marking with the eagles contained in a black-ringed disc (Crown copyright)

BOTTOM LEFT
Lightning T.5 (XS451/'X') of No 11 Sqn entered service in 1965 at Binbrook. On 25 November 1976, this aircraft made its last flight when it was delivered to RAF St Athan. In early 1979 it was moved to RAF Newton and housed in the missile museum, where it's used by post-graduate trainees. The aircraft wears LTF markings and is serialed 8503M

BELOW
Lightning T.5 (XS452/'Y') of No 11 Sqn in trial dark green camouflage at Binbrook, 26 September 1975. Yellow code letter, and yellow-edged black eagles

(8,046 km). In January 1969 the squadron deployed to Tengah in Singapore, staging through Muharraq and Gan.

Throughout its time at Leuchars the squadron was involved in many NATO exchanges and the whole gamut of air defence exercises. Several of these involved the Royal Navy since the RAF had taken on responsibility for air defence of the Fleet. As well as routine tasks, there were special events such as the flypast for the Prince of Wales' Investiture on 1 July 1969 and a two-aircraft display at the Paris Air Show in 1971.

On 22 March 1972 the squadron moved south to its new home at Binbrook, handing over its air defence duties at Leuchars to Phantom FG.1s of No 43 Sqn. In June 1972, it deployed to Akrotiri to relieve No 56 Sqn for one month while the Cyprus-based squadron completed armament practice camp (APC) at Valley. With the addition of three Lightning F.3s to the unit's strength more emphasis was given to the air combat mission.

In 1973, the first fuel crisis forced flying restrictions upon the squadron and 'C' Flight was formed in 1974 to carry out conversion training when No 226 OCU at Coltishall closed. Some of the Lightnings were transferred to 'C' Flight at

Binbrook in the grip of winter, but it's business as usual. Lightning T.5 (XS458/'BT') taxies past LTF T.5, 'DT'. Flt Lt G G Howe, an intercept weapons instructor (IWI), has just completed a 'check ride' to test a junior pilot on intercept procedures

TOP RIGHT
Lightning F.6s (XS901/'BJ' and XS927/'BH') of No 11 Sqn on the same flight line at Binbrook

Binbrook. 'C' Flight became an independent Lightning Training Flight (LTF) in 1975, when the aeroplane's operational life was extended.

The invasion of Cyprus in 1974 caused the deployment of six aircraft to Akrotiri in January. There was no action for No 11 Sqn but the pilots maintained readiness from dawn to dusk each day. Between April and August 1976, the squadron detached to Leconfield whilst Binbrook's runway was resurfaced. On 3 August 1979 No 11 Sqn took part in festivals to mark the 25th anniversary of the Lightning.

Another view of 'BA', this time with white overwing tanks

Lightning F.6 (XR725/'BA') of No 11 Sqn landing at Binbrook, May 1983

No 19 Sqn

Motto: *Possunt quia posse videntur* (They can because they think they can)

No 19 Sqn is one of only two RAF squadrons to have operated the F.2 version of the Lightning and its successor, the F.2A, a distinction which it shared with No 92 Sqn. The unit had many notable firsts: It was first to be equipped with the French Spad (S.VII), and was also the first to receive Spitfires in 1938. It was also the first to receive the Lightning F.2.

By the end of 1962 the squadron converted from the Hunter F.6 to the Lightning, and received its first F.2, XN775, on December 17. The F.2 was a vast improvement over the F.1A, with an improved reheat system, longer range and more advanced electronic equipment which enhanced the aircraft's all-weather capability. The only other front-line unit to get F.2s was No 92 Sqn and these two units became known as the Leconfield Wing.

By mid-April, twelve aircraft were on strength and by the summer No 19 Sqn was fully operational with their new mounts. The following year the squadron began concentrating on ground attack work with the four nose-mounted cannon.

1965 proved to be a very busy year. In January No 19 Sqn participated in the State Funeral of Sir Winston Churchill, taking part in the formation flypast and providing one officer to 'Keep the Vigil' during the Lying-in-State.

No 19 Sqn was then chosen to take part in the trials with the Victor K.1 flight refuelling tankers, with the object of increasing the Lightnings' on-station duration and enhance their overseas deployment capability.

By the autumn the squadron had chalked up another first, when on 23 September 1965 it was transferred from Fighter Command to RAF Germany to be part of NATO's missile and fighter defences and moved from Leconfield to Gütersloh, where it became the RAF's first supersonic squadron in the Second Allied Tactical Air Force (TWOATAF). The squadron took some time to settle in and did not become fully operational until early the following year.

Towards the end of 1966 the F.2s were modified and re-issued to the Gütersloh squadrons as F.2As. No 19 Sqn received its first F.2A in February 1968 and deliveries continued throughout the next 18 months. The converted aircraft looked like the F.6, featuring the large

Squadron photograph taken at RAF Gütersloh in June 1968. No 19 Sqn pilots relax on the wing of XN777/'K', a Lightning F.2A. At rear left of picture, F.2 XN774/'C' prior to conversion. The three F.2As carry Firestreaks— this mark was not compatible with Red Top (Crown copyright)

OPPOSITE
Lightning F.2A (XN776/'C') of No 19 Sqn next to target facilities Lightning F.1A XM173. This F.2A is preserved at the Museum of Flight at East Fortune

Lightning F.2 (XN782/'K') of No 19 Sqn at RAF Gutersloh, West Germany, in the mid-1960s. The aircraft is armed with 4 × 30 mm Aden cannons (two in ventral weapons pack). The squadron badge is a red and green inverted dolphin on a white oval in a black and yellow laurel. White and blue checks

BELOW
Toned-down T-bird of No 19 Sqn in NATO dark green finish. Lightning T.4 XM973/'V' with code letter repeated on main wheel door

No 23 Sqn now operates the Phantom FGR.2, based at RAF Stanley in the Falkland Islands. The Phantom has re-equipped nearly all the previous Lightning squadrons save Nos 5 and 11 Sqns at Binbrook. No 74 Sqn, the first front-line unit to operate the Lightning, will be re-formed on the F-4J(UK) in 1985. Picture taken from Hercules C.1(K)
(Jeremy Flack, API)

ventral fuel tank, cambered leading edge wing, fin and arrester hook, with the added advantage of retaining the nose-mounted Aden cannons. However, the F.2A was not compatible with the Red Top missile.

From 1973 onwards, the Lightnings of Nos 19 and 92 Sqns were toned down and NATO dark green camouflage was applied to the upper surfaces of the aircraft.

The squadron continued with its low-level CAP role and Battle Flight readiness over the next two years, but the RAF's re-equipment programme saw the Jaguar coming into squadron service. Phantoms were therefore released for the air superiority role and the Lightning began to be phased-out. On 27 September 1976, the first Phantom for No 19 Sqn arrived at Wildenrath. On 31 December 1976, No 19 (Air Defence-Lightning) Sqn disbanded at RAF Gütersloh. The following day No 19 (Designate) Sqn (Air Defence-Phantom) at RAF Wildenrath took over the number plate.

No 23 Sqn
Motto: *Semper aggressus* (Always attacking)

No 23 Sqn flew the Lightning for over a decade and it received the last Lightning to be delivered to the RAF, XS938, on 28 August 1967. No 23 Sqn—the 'Red Eagles'—were based at Leuchars in Scotland for almost all of their association with the Lightning.

In April 1959 the squadron received Javelin FAW.7s, equipped with Firestreaks, and returned to Coltishall, only to move (yet again) to Horsham-St-Faith in March 1960. By June 1960 the squadron had converted to Javelin FAW.9s, which had an air-to-air refuelling capability. In the same month it fired its first missile during practice at Valley. The squadron returned to Coltishall in July and took part in several deployments during the last six months of the year. Eight aircraft flew to Karachi in June 1961, using air-to-air refuelling en route, and shortly afterwards the squadron was deployed to Nicosia for four weeks during the Kuwait crisis. In August the squadron moved to Horsham-St-Faith, only to return to Coltishall in October. In October 1962 three of its aircraft set a record by flying non-stop to Aden, and in December it was the first unit in Fighter Command to flight-refuel at night. It also practised its overseas reinforcement role in January 1963 by flying to Tengah for a month-long detachment.

TOP
Lightning F.1A (XM169/'W') wearing No 23 Sqn markings, in a forlorn state as an airfield decoy at RAF Leuchars in the mid-1970s

Lightning F.3 (XP752/'O') of No 23 'Red Eagle' Sqn landing at Leuchars in about 1967. A small squadron badge consisting of a red eagle on a white disc is worn on the fin

In March No 23 Sqn ended a 14-year association with Coltishall when it moved to Leuchars, and in August 1964 it started to re-equip with Lightning F.3s. The first Lightnings, XP707 and '708, arrived on the 18th of the month. Early in 1965 the squadron's brilliantly coloured aircraft took part in flight refuelling exercises using USAF KC-135 tankers.

The Squadron won the Dacre Trophy for proficiency in weapon training in May 1967, the same month it received the first of its interim F.6s. A few weeks later the full production F.6s began to arrive, but it was not until the autumn that the squadron received its full complement of twelve Lightning F.6s.

Live scrambles to intercept Soviet long range reconnaissance aircraft became a fairly common feature of the squadron's work. In August 1968 the No 23 Sqn made the news when two Lightnings, XR725/'A' and XS936/'B', participated in the Canadian International Air Show in Toronto. The two Lightnings flew there non-stop using in-flight refuelling in 7 hours 20 minutes. The two aircraft returned to Leuchars for a champagne welcome on September 3. That same month the squadron became operational with the Red Top missile. During December, Sqn Ldr N D McEwen completed 1,000 hours on Lightnings and became the first member of the unit to do so.

No 23 Sqn won the Dacre trophy for the second time in June 1969 and again in 1975, and also won the Aberporth Trophy in 1970 and 1971. Overseas detachments included visits to Beauvechain in Belgium in July 1969, Malta in April 1970 (the latter was the first *full* squadron deployment for five years) and Sweden in September 1970. The unit was the first RAF fighter squadron to visit Sweden for over ten years and to celebrate all the aircraft were decorated with a new red eagle emblem on the fin; and in February 1971 the squadron deployed to Akrotiri to practise the air defence of Cyprus and air combat-manoeuvring (ACM).

Twin 30 mm Aden gun packs were fitted to the Lightnings and on 26 March 1971 the first trial shots were carried out with complete success. The heavy QRA commitment continued.

On 31 October 1975, No 23 Sqn disbanded its Lightning element at Leuchars and the aircraft were re-allocated to Binbrook with the exception of a single machine, which was given to No 56

Lightning F.6 of No 23 Sqn pacing a Tupolev Tu-142 Bear-D (probably AV-MF) high over the North Sea in 1975. XR753/'F' carries a small Canadian flag in front of the red and dark blue nose bars. This aircraft is currently operated by No 5 Sqn as 'AG' (Crown copyright)

Lightning F.6 (XS938/'E') of No 23 Sqn was the last F.6 delivered to the RAF. It crashed on 4 March 1971

Sqn at Wattisham in early 1976. Phantom FGR.2s of No 111 Sqn took over the role of No 23 Sqn at Leuchars. No 23 Sqn re-formed at Coningsby on 17 November 1975, equipped with Phantom FGR.2s, and later moved to Wattisham on 25 February 1976.

Lightning F.6 (XR760/'H') of No 23 Sqn unsticks in 'burner. This aircraft is still in service. (See pages 52–53 and 56)

Working up to operational standard on the newly acquired Lightnings was a relatively speedy task for the squadron, completed by August of 1967. It was in this month that the now well-known 'Triplex' markings were unveiled. The squadron spray guns had been out and the Lightning fin displayed the squadron insignia of an eagle preying on a buzzard, and either side of the nose roundel, three red crosses in a white rectangle outlined in red.

In September 1967, Wg Cdr L W Phipps took over the squadron from Sqn Ldr L A Boyer. No 29 Sqn remained a top squadron in Fighter Command until April 1968, when Fighter Command was merged with Bomber Command to form Strike Command. On this occasion the squadron supplied three aircraft for the 'Demise Flypast' to commemorate the passing of Fighter Command. That same month, the squadron flew a wing formation of twelve aircraft over Ipswich to celebrate the fiftieth anniversary of the Royal Air Force.

Throughout its time at Wattisham No 29 Sqn was involved in several exchange exercises to such places as Neuberg in West Germany, Dijon in France, Ørland in Norway and Grosseto in Italy. The squadron then suffered a double tragedy when XP698 and XP747 collided over the North Sea while on a night exercise on 16 February 1972. That same year No 29 Sqn flew 2,000 commemorative first day covers from Cambrai in France to England for the RAF Museum—which was to benefit by the sale of the covers to philatelic enthusiasts all over the world.

No 29 Sqn notched up another first on 19 July 1974, when it received the Dacre trophy (awarded annually by the Air Officer Commanding No 11 Group, RAF Strike Command) for making the most significant contribution to overall fighter efficiency during the year (including missile practice camp, flight safety, aircraft serviceability and response to alert exercises).

With the release of Phantoms for air defence duties the F.3 was phased out, and on 31 December 1974 the No 29 Sqn number plate changed hands during a ceremonial parade at RAF Wattisham. The parade was commanded by Wg Cdr John D C Hawtin, the retiring OC of No 29 Sqn who had been in command since June 1973. The incoming OC was Wg Cdr B W 'Danny' Lavender. The squadron moved to RAF Coningsby and re-equipped with the Phantom FGR.2—its four Sparrow, four Sidewinder and gun combination offering a greatly improved air defence capability. In the late 1980s, No 29 Sqn is to be the first Tornado F.2 unit.

No 29 Sqn

Motto: *Impiger et acer* (Energetic and keen)

In May 1967, No 29 Sqn exchanged its Javelins for Lightnings and for the first time since 1935 became a single-seat fighter squadron. It was the last unit to form on the Lightning and its seven-year association with the F.3 was spent at Wattisham.

The squadron re-equipped with Javelin FAW.6s at the end of 1957. In 1963 it left Fighter Command to become the all-weather component of Near East Air Force in Cyprus. The squadron was fairly mobile during its stay there, moving to various parts of the NEAF area, and in 1964 the squadron was sent to Zambia during the Rhodesian crisis.

In May 1967, No 29 Sqn was relieved by the Lightnings of No 56 Sqn and returned to the UK to become part of Fighter Command once more, re-equipping with Lightning F.3s at RAF Wattisham. The squadron's first Lightning, a T.5 (XV328) from No 60 MU, arrived on May 10 followed by the F.3s, which had previously served at Leuchars with No 74 Sqn, who had traded them in for Lightning F.6s. For the first time since 1935 No 29 Sqn became a single-seat fighter squadron with the F.3.

LEFT
*Lightning F.3 (XR718/'C') of No 29 Sqn showing live
Red Top missile with protective cover removed. The
squadron badge depicts a red eagle diving on a yellow
buzzard within a white disc with a red border. The nose
bars are red and white. XR718 saw service with No 5 Sqn
as 'AS'*

BOTTOM LEFT
*Landing shot of Lightning F.3 (XP765/'A') shows the
early markings used by No 29 Sqn's Lightnings. The nose
bars flanking the roundel were later elongated. XP765 was
scrapped at Wattisham in 1975*

BELOW
*Lightning T.5 (XS422/'O') of No 29 Sqn with the late
Kenneth More (probably best remembered for his part in
the movie 'Reach For The Sky') in the right-hand seat
(Grimsby Evening Telegraph)*

*Lightning F.3s of No 29 Sqn at RAF Luqa, Malta, May
1969
(Godfrey Mangion)*

*Gutted Lightning F.3 (XP763/'P') formerly with No 29
Sqn, on the Wattisham dump in 1975. Ex-No 111 Sqn
F.3 (XP759/'F') lies beyond*

TOP
*Lightning T.5 (XV328/'Z') of No 29 Sqn about to
touchdown at RAF Wattisham. This was the first
Lightning accepted by the squadron, being delivered on 10
May 1967. It now serves with the LTF at Binbrook as
'DY'. See page 136*

No 56 Sqn
Motto: *Quid si coelum ruat* (What if heaven falls)

No 56 Sqn will always be remembered as a Lightning unit, their spell as the official Fighter Command aerobatic team—the 'Firebirds'—and flamboyant markings being just two reasons. It was also one of two units to have operated three versions of the Lightning, namely the F.1A, F.3 and F.6.

On 27 April 1956, the squadron was honoured with the presentation of its standard by HRH The Duchess of Kent. The squadron then visited Malta in June 1957, returning to Waterbeach early in July. In November 1958, the Hunter F.5s gave way to F.6s. Moving to Wattisham in July 1959, the squadron was detached to Cyprus in August and September of that year.

No 56 Sqn converted to the Lightning from the Hunter F.6 to become the RAF's second Lightning squadron and took delivery of the first F.1A (XM172) at Wattisham in December 1960. The squadron progressively received its full complement of Lightnings and by March 1961, XM172 to 183 inclusive had been accepted.

The squadron's work-up to operational status with their new mounts began at Wattisham, but continued at Coltishall while the runway at Wattisham underwent major repair work.

Lightning F.1A (XM182/'M') of No 56 Sqn at Wattisham in 1962 behind a row of Gloster Javelin FAW.8s of No 41 Sqn. XM182 flew with the 'Firebirds' aerobatic team (note injector nozzle for smoke-making oil over lower jetpipe), and had a red spine and fin with phoenix rising from red fire within a white, black-edged disc. Large red and white checks on nose and rakish national marking on leading edge of fin. Code letter black with white outline
(BAe)

Lightning F.3 (XP701/'W') of No 56 Sqn at Wattisham
in late 1960s with large phoenix rising from orange and red
shaded fire

During 1965 No 56 Sqn introduced this spectacular scheme on the Lightning F.3. Red spine leading to checkerboard red and white fin, red and white arrowheads in front of roundel with detail of phoenix, and red code letter 'D' edged in white located on the airbrake. This is XR719

OPPOSITE
The Firebird's Lightning T.4 (XM989/'X') which was converted into a T.54 and sold to Saudi Arabia

In 1962 the squadron was first to use the Lightning F.1A for air-to-air refuelling with Valiant tankers. No 56 Sqn conducted intensive trials and in July a detachment flew non-stop from Wattisham to Akrotiri, Cyprus, for a major exercise.

The Firebirds were formed in 1963 and superseded the 'Blue Diamonds' when the latter team stood down to convert from Hunters to Lightnings. Their Lightnings were specially adorned with distinctive red markings—red fin, spine and wing and tailplane leading edges and a red and white checkerboard astride the roundel. The Firebirds were coded in serial number order, XM171/'A', XM172/'B' etc. Full use was made of the Lightning's power to demonstrate its rocket-like climb and agility. XM179/'J' was lost after a mid-air collision while practising aerobatics on 6 June 1963. The other aircraft involved, XM174/'D', made a safe landing.

In April 1965, No 56 Sqn, along with 'Treble-One', traded in their F.1As for Lightning F.3s. The F.1As were transferred to No 226 OCU at Coltishall and target facilities flights.

Within a few weeks of taking delivery of the F.3 No 56 Sqn surpassed themselves and applied a colour scheme to beat all colour schemes. They adorned the entire fin and rudder with a red-and-white checkerboard and applied red-and-white arrowheads on the nose. Similar colour schemes were soon adopted by other Lightning squadrons, but were toned down later in the year. The mass of paint caused drag and was difficult to preserve—weathering of the colour scheme was severe after supersonic missions.

In September 1965, No 56 Sqn took part in 'Unison 65' and during this exercise XP765 was displayed at RAF Cranwell with dummy overwing tanks. The following year the squadron took part in the Malta air defence exercise 'Adex 66'.

During April 1967 the Lightnings of No 56 Sqn moved to the Mediterranean to replace the Javelins of No 29 Sqn at Akrotiri, Cyprus, and assumed the air defence responsibilities for the strategically placed island. No 29 Sqn returned to take No 56's place at Wattisham and re-formed on the Lightning. No 56 Sqn flew the F.3 in Cyprus for four years until September 1971, when it exchanged them for F.6s. When No 74 Sqn disbanded at Tengah, Singapore, in August 1971, its F.6's were flown to Cyprus and No 56 Sqn re-equipped with them in September. The squadron's F.3s were sent home, mainly to No 60 MU for re-distribution. The Lightning F.6, with its greater fuel capacity and endurance, improved the squadrons' operational capability and it continued to protect British Sovereign Base Area airspace for the next three years. During the Turkish invasion of Cyprus in 1974 about 200 operational sorties were flown by the squadron.

In January 1975 the RAF units on the island were withdrawn and No 56 Sqn returned to Wattisham. The first five Lightnings arrived on January 21 and were followed by two more on the 22nd and the remaining six on the 30th, the T.5 XS452/'X' being left at Akrotiri for the use of visiting detachments. The three Canberras of No 56 Sqn also returned. They were used by the unit to provide their own target facilities—an impractical task for UK based aircraft.

No 56 Sqn operated the Lightning for another eighteen months. In June 1975, No 56 Sqn celebrated its Diamond Jubilee and recorded another first for the squadron—the presentation of the Dacre Trophy. The trophy is in memory of F/O Kenneth Dacre, DFC, who was killed

Immaculate Lightning T.5 (XS456/'X') of No 56 Sqn about to land at RAF Akrotiri, Cyprus, in 1972. XS456 currently serves with the LTF at Binbrook as 'DT'. See page 64

Two Lightning F.6s with overwing tanks from No 56 Sqn on finals. XR728/'D' (nearest) and XS932/'J'

piloting a No 605 squadron Mosquito on one of the first intruder patrols over Germany.

On June 4 there was a fly-past of four Lightnings carrying 13,000 stamp covers commemorating Capt Albert Ball, VC, the famous World War I ace who flew with No 56 Sqn.

Later in the month, on June 28, No 56 Sqn (Air Defence-Lightning) disbanded at Wattisham and the following day No 56 (Designate) Sqn re-formed on the Phantom FGR.2 at RAF Coningsby. On 22 March 1976 the Phantoms moved south to Wattisham to take over No 56 Sqn's number plate and fulfil Strike Command's commitment in the southern sector of the interceptor alert force. No 56 Sqn's Lightnings were taken over by the Binbrook Wing. This change-over marked the last of the four UK-based Lightning squadrons to be converted to Phantoms, although two Lightning squadrons, Nos 5 and 11, remain operational at Binbrook.

TOP RIGHT
Late production Lightning F.6 (XS933/'K') of No 56 Sqn departs RAF Luqa, Malta, equipped with overwing tanks for the return flight to Wattisham in 1973 (Godfrey Mangion)

No 74 Sqn
Motto: I Fear No Man

In 1960, No 74 Sqn—'The Tiger Squadron'—was the first RAF front-line squadron to receive the Lightning. The squadron also had the distinction of being the only operational unit to be equipped with the F.1 version of the Lightning. Only Nos 74 and 56 Sqns were equipped with three Lightning marks: No 74 Sqn had the F.1, F.3, and F.6.

The squadron provided an aerobatic team of four Hunters for several displays in 1959, and continued to fly this type until July 1960, when No 74 Sqn was selected to be the first squadron to receive the Lightning, based at RAF Coltishall.

No 74 Sqn took on strength its first Lightning F.1, XM165, on 29 June 1960. The Lightning, with its primary armament of two Firestreak infrared homing air-to-air missiles, was the RAF's first all-weather integrated weapons system, and presented a formidable conversion task for the pilots of No 74 Sqn, who now had a mount that had a top speed double the one they were trading in. Nevertheless, No 74 Sqn, with the help of the Central Fighter Establishment's Lightning Conversion Unit, converted from their Hunter F.6s to the Lightning with few problems and at

the 1960 Farnborough Air Show, Sqn Ldr J F G Howe, then commanding the squadron, led formation flypasts of four aircraft.

With its full complement of twelve fighters, the normal establishment for Lightning squadrons, No 74 Sqn became operational early in 1961 and by the time of the Paris Air Show in June the squadron was flying an aerobatic team of nine aircraft. At the Farnborough Air Show in September the squadron gave the first public demonstration of nine Lightnings rolling in tight formation. In 1962, under its new CO, Sqn Ldr P G Botterill, No 74 Sqn was selected as Fighter Command's leading aerobatic team and named the 'Tigers'.

In June 1963 several of the squadron's F.1s were handed over to No 60 MU, and the remaining aircraft were supplemented by ex-AFDS aircraft. At that time F.1 strength was down to ten aircraft, although these were up-dated by the inclusion of new equipment, including UHF radios.

On 28 February 1964, the squadron moved to its new base at Leuchars in Scotland, and two months later began to re-equip with Lightning F.3s, the first of which was XP700, arriving on April 14. The squadron's old F.1s went to No 226 OCU and a few to No 111 Sqn to keep the latter

Tyger, Tyger, burning bright
In the forests of the night.
What immortal hand or eye
Could frame thy fearful symmetry?
Lightning F.1 of No 74 Sqn (XM145/'Q') on engine test
at Warton in 1960. (With apologies to William Blake)

OVERLEAF
*Nine Lightning F.1s of No 74 'Tiger' Sqn practise their
station keeping
(BAe)*

No 74 Sqn began to re-equip with the Lightning F.3 in April 1964. XP700/'A' crashed on 7 August 1973 when on the strength of No 29 Sqn

unit up to strength. The 'Tigers' quickly adapted to their new mounts but on August 28 tragedy struck when XP704/'H' crashed while practising for a forthcoming Battle of Britain display.

On 3 June 1965, Princess Margaret visited Leuchars to present a standard to No 74 Sqn. That same year saw an increase in the number of Soviet reconnaissance aircraft probing UK air space and the Lightnings were kept busy. The interceptions took place well out over the North Sea and it was necessary for Victor tankers to be on hand to compensate for the limited endurance of the F.3—the squadron re-equipped with this Mark in May 1964.

The 'Tigers' were the first squadron to receive the definitive F.6 when XR768/'A' began the replacement of the F.3s in August 1966. At the 1966 Farnborough Air Show, XR770 wore a spurious Saudi Arabian serial '53-770' to publicize a recent order from that Middle East country.

The improved range and endurance of the F.6 was welcome, but the change-over took many weeks and the squadron had to persevere with F.3s until the New Year. During March 1967 the squadron took part in trials with the arrester hook and Rotary Hydraulic Arrester Gear (RHAG). The trials were undertaken in conjunction with BAC.

During their stay at Leuchars No 74 Sqn was host to the annual 'Tiger Meet'. This event, first held in 1961, features a number of squadrons from NATO countries who have the common bond of the tiger as their squadron emblem. The object of the Meet is to further the mutual understanding of roles, aircraft and operational procedures, both on the ground and in the air, by professional and social liaison.

In June 1967 the squadron moved from Leuchars to Tengah, Singapore, to replace the Javelins of No 64 Sqn—exercise 'Hydraulic'. On June 4, six Lightnings took-off for Tengah led by the CO, Wg Cdr 'Ken' Goodwin; the following day five more departed and the last two left on the 6th. The Lightnings arrived safely in Tengah after making planned stops at Akrotiri Cyprus, Masirah Persian Gulf, and Gan, the RAF's former remote island base in the Indian Ocean, and the aircraft were in-flight refuelled by a total of seventeen Victor tankers of Nos 55, 57 and 214 Sqns based at Marham. All thirteen Lightnings were fully operational by June 12. This was the largest in-flight refuelling operation the RAF had mounted to date, and the furthest distance a Lightning aircraft had flown. The T.5 trainer (XS416) remained behind and XV329 was shipped from Sydenham, Belfast, to Tengah instead.

It was necessary to send the T-bird by sea because it had insufficient range (no overwing tanks) to accompany the unit on its flight-refuelled journey to the Far East. After the disbandment of the squadron in August 1971, XV329 returned by sea. Back at Sydenham in December it was discovered that acid spillage from the batteries had corroded the airframe and it was written-off.

No 74 was the only RAF air defence squadron in the Far East Air Force. The squadron took part in several air defence exercises, the main one being exercise 'Town House'. On 16 June 1969, four of the aircraft flew 2,000 (3,218 km) miles non-stop from Singapore to Darwin to participate in one of the biggest air defence exercises ever held in Australia. In all, about 50 aircraft from three nations, including RAF Canberras, Vulcans and RAAF Mirages, took part in the exercise which ended on June 26.

Three months later four Lightnings from the squadron flew non-stop to Darwin again, but they stayed for only two days. The previous month the squadron had been involved in exercise 'Bersatu Padu', a five-nation exercise held in Singapore and Western Malaya. A pair of Lightnings also flew to Thailand to take part in a static display in Bangkok.

The British Forces then began to pull-out of the Far East and after more than four years' service with the Far East Air Force, No 74 (Trinidad) Sqn disbanded on 25 August 1971. One of the more off-beat incidents during the squadron's stay at Tengah involved a large python which wound itself around the nosewheel of a taxying Lightning and then crawled into the wheel bay. Squadron groundcrew and locally employed labourers tried in vain to haul the python out. Not until the airmen played fire extinguishers into the bay did the snake release its tenacious hold. Another hectic struggle followed before the snake was safely imprisoned in a wooden box. The final task of the 'Tiger' pilots in the Far East was to fly from Tengah to Akrotiri, Cyprus, where the aircraft were absorbed by No 56 Sqn. The Lightnings were staged through Gan, and Muharraq in the Persian gulf and each of the Lightnings were

The Tiger's T-bird, a Lightning T.4 (XM974/'T'), which later crashed while being operated by No 226 OCU on 14 December 1972. Yellow day-glo band on rear fuselage overlaps fin

Lightning F.3s of No 74 Sqn lined-up at RAF Leuchars on a wet, dismal day in 1964. All six aircraft wear the standard uniform of a No 74 Sqn F.3: black spine and fin, large tiger with black/yellow face, white teeth, and red tongue mounted on a white disc, sweptback national marking with yellow border, yellow code letter, and yellow/black roundel bars. The nearest aircraft, (XP752/'D') collided with a Mirage III on 20 May 1971, but landed safely. XP704/'H' crashed near Leuchars on 28 August 1964, killing the pilot. XP698/'F' crashed into the North Sea on 16 February 1972 after a collision with XP747
(BAe)

OPPOSITE
Lightning F.3 (XP755/'P') of No 74 Sqn in overall natural metal with small tiger insignia on fin. This aircraft was scrapped at Leconfield in 1975
(BAe)

BELOW
Lightning F.6 (XR769/'B') of No 74 Sqn wearing the final scheme adopted by the unit; black fin with small tiger insignia on fin

*Lightning T.4 (XM995/'T') of No 92 Sqn en route for
engine run-ups, probably at Leconfield in 1963. Blue spine
and fin, red/yellow arrow behind roundel, and a yellow
day-glo band on the rear fuselage. The ventral tank has
been removed. This aircraft later became a decoy at
Wildenrath, serialled 8542M*

flight-refuelled seven times by Victor tankers.
They touched down in Akrotiri after thirteen
hours of flying.

At the disbandment parade at Tengah, reviewed
by the Commander Far East Air Force, Air Vice
Marshal Nigel Maynard, there was a flypast of
four Lightnings as the general salute was given. A
single Lightning then flew over the parade at dusk
as the squadron standard was marched off the
parade ground in slow time—closing another
chapter in the illustrious history of No 74 Sqn.
The squadron is due to re-form in 1985 and will
be equipped with 15 McDonnell Douglas F-4J
(UK) Phantoms purchased from US Navy stocks.

No 92 Sqn
Motto: *Aut pugna aut morere* (Either fight or die)

No 92 Sqn was the only other front-line unit to
receive the F.2 and F.2A versions of the
Lightning—first at Leconfield and then in RAF
Germany. The squadron badge consists of two
maple leaves and a striking cobra, symbolizing its
association with East India in World War II.

No 92 Sqn converted from the Hunter F.6 to
the Lightning F.2 in April 1963. Unfortunately
the change-over also meant the demise of the 'Blue
Diamonds' aerobatic team.

The squadron received its first Lightning,
XN783/'A' on 17 April 1963 and followed a
similar course to No 19 Sqn to become operational
again in the summer. During 1964 the squadron
was engaged in ground attack training pending its
move to Germany. That same year the squadron's
blue-finned Lightnings provided Fighter
Command's aerobatic team and put the Lightning
through its paces at the Farnborough Air Show.

In April 1964, XN785 ran out of fuel while on

Lightning F.2 (XN731/'M') of No 92 Sqn at low-level over Leconfield. Became decoy at Laarbruch, serialled 8518M

Lightning F.6 (XS893/'G') of No 74 Sqn with overwing tanks at RAF Tengah in June 1967 during exercise 'Hydraulic'. The unit was deployed from Wattisham to replace Javelin FAW.9s of No 64 Sqn. XS893 crashed at Tengah on 12 August 1970

Lightning F.2A (XN780/'K') of No 92 Sqn at Gütersloh, about 1971. Blue spine/fin and red/yellow checks on nose. The fin insignia is an orange cobra with a brown branch and leaves on a white disc (MAP)

TOP
Lightning F.2A (XN732/'R') of No 92 Sqn at Gütersloh.
Tigercat missile battery in background

Camouflaged Lightning decoys at Gutersloh in 1977

TOP
Lightning T.4 (XM968/'Q') of No 92 Sqn in NATO dark green scheme. XM968 crashed on 24 February 1977, shortly before the squadron disbanded

The Phantom represented a huge leap in capability—two-crew, 4 × Sparrow AIM-7E-2, 4 × Sidewinder AIM-9D, and centreline SUU-23/A cannon. No 19 Sqn FGR.2 in company with Harrier GR.3
(Crown copyright)

Shabby Lightning F.2A (XN778/'A') ex-No 92 Sqn on decoy duty at Wildenrath in January 1983. Formerly the OC's machine, a crown appears above the cobra and the words KING COBRA flank the white disc, with two 'diamonds' below it

RIGHT
Tailpiece: Lightning T.4 XM995 (see page 96) with inscription: 'The last Lightning T.4 reheat pipe "kicked" into place this day 6 April 1977 AD (after disbandment)'. 'The Lads' were Chuck Lundie, Ron Pepper, Colin Thomas, Al Smith, Don MacLellan, and Simon Randle (ancilliary). Recognition experts will find and identify a Gazelle AH.1 with underslung load

approach to Leconfield after an abortive flight-refuelling exercise with a Valiant. The pilot attempted to land at Hutton Cranswick, a disused World War II fighter airfield, but the aircraft crashed. A replacement aircraft, XN768, arrived from store at No 33 MU to keep the squadron up to strength.

With the arrival of XN769 in August 1965 and XN794 in October the squadron increased its strength and in December 1965 it moved to Germany to form part of the NATO's Second Allied Tactical Air Force (TWOATAF), within Allied Air Forces Central Europe. Its first base in Germany was at RAF Geilenkirchen to take over the air defence responsibilities of the Javelin-equipped No 11 Sqn. Inherent in this move was a change in emphasis in the squadron's role because as part of the post-war Tri-National Agreement, Britain, America, and France undertook to police West German air space; the squadron had to maintain a battle flight of aircraft on instant readiness at all times. No 92 Sqn kept its colourful fins for a short time, but the Lightning squadrons in Germany were subsequently toned down by the addition of NATO dark green camouflage. In December 1965, No 92 Sqn was presented with its standard: it was fitting that the reviewing officer was Air Chief Marshal Sir James Robb, who, as the senior flight commander in 1918, shot down the first enemy aircraft credited to the squadron.

In January 1968 the squadron moved eastwards to RAF Gütersloh to enable it to react more quickly to any intrusion into West German airspace. In July it received its first F.2A and had re-equipped completely by March 1973. The squadron flew two types of missions, low level to the east of the Möhne Dam and high level over the 'clutch' airfields of Wildenrath, Laarbruck and Brüggen. The sorties were mostly flown visually because the radar was comparatively ineffective low down. The average scramble time was only $3\frac{1}{2}$ minutes. Low-altitude CAP work was done with Buccaneers and Harriers. The Lightnings flew against a variety of opposition ranging from

Luftwaffe Fiat G.91s to Bitburg-based F-15 Eagles.

With the introduction of the Jaguar into RAF service, many of the Phantom FGR.2s previously tasked with ground attack, strike and reconnaissance duties were made available for air defence. The Phantom is greatly superior to the Lightning in the air defence role by virtue of its greater endurance, long-range pulse-doppler radar, and an air-to-air missile armament four times greater than any Lightning. Many Phantom crews would also argue that the addition of a navigator is a vital life preserver in air combat.

On 3 January 1977, No 92 (Designate) Sqn was re-formed at RAF Wildenrath with a nucleus of experienced Phantom aviators and two or three 'first tour' navigators. A quote from the official history of No 92 Sqn at the time indicates the esteem in which the Designate unit held its forebears: 'The squadron to a man is enthusiastic to prove its worth as a front line unit and also to ensure that the traditional spirit and excellence of No 92 Sqn is maintained.' On Friday, 1 April 1977 the squadron's standard was officially handed over at a parade at RAF Gütersloh and No 92 Sqn was now a Phantom squadron based at RAF Wildenrath. Its old Lightnings were relegated to the role of decoys or scrapped.

Decaying F.2A XN775/'B' (ex-No 92 Sqn) in use as a decoy at Gutersloh

OVERLEAF
Two Lightning F.3s of No 111 'Treble One' Sqn ready for take-off at RAF Akrotiri in the late 1960s. The aircraft at right of picture, XP758/'S', was scrapped at Leconfield in 1975

No 111 Sqn
Motto: *Adstantes* (Standing by)

No 111 Sqn—'Treble One'—became the third
Lightning squadron and thereby relinquished its
role as the world's premier aerobatic team. Known
as the 'Black Arrows' the team had achieved
world-wide fame with its all black Hunters.

'Treble One' started to re-equip at Wattisham in
1958. In April 1961 the squadron started to
convert to the Lightning F.1A and received
XM184 to 192 and XM213 to 216. It was the
third and last of the F.1/F.1A squadrons. The last
F.1A to be built (XM216) was delivered to No 111
Sqn as 'P' in August.

The Lightning F.1A had provision for flight
refuelling and No 111 Sqn deployed to Cyprus,
Libya, Germany and Malta. New squadron
markings now appeared on the aircraft; a yellow-
edged black Lightning flash either side of the nose,
with the squadron badge on the tail. The tail was
also painted black on some aircraft.

In May 1964, a six-minute record turnround of
four Lightnings was achieved at a demonstration
for SACEUR. In January 1965, re-equipped with
Lightning F.3s, the squadron formed the leading
box in a formation of sixteen aircraft for a final
salute and flypast over the funeral barge of Sir
Winston Churchill.

August 1967 saw 'Treble One's' 50th
anniversary and a flying display which has rarely
been equalled. The display included a Bristol
Fighter, Hurricane, Spitfire, Meteor, Hunter and
Lightning; all former squadron aircraft.

The RAF celebrated its 50th anniversary in
April 1968. At Wattisham the event was celebrated
by Lightning aircraft flying low and rather fast
flypasts over most of the large towns in Suffolk. A
total of twenty aircraft took part, all in box fours.

With Phantoms being withdrawn to the UK for
air defence duties the Lightning F.3 squadrons
were steadily phased out. The first Lightning
squadron to receive the Phantom was 'Treble
One'. July 1974 saw the formation of No 111
(Designate) Sqn as a No 11 Group lodger unit at
Coningsby flying Phantom FGR.2s. This moved
to Leuchars in November 1975. On 30 September
1974 at a ceremony at Wattisham the squadron
standard was handed over to the new Phantom
squadron.

*Lightning F.1A (XM192/'K') of No 111 Sqn landing at
Wattisham in 1961. The Lightning flash is black, edged
yellow, and the tail insignia is three black sea axes crossed
by two red swords—there were many variations
(Flight)*

OPPOSITE AND BOTTOM LEFT
Lightning F.3 (XR711/'A') of No 111 Sqn overshot the runway at Wattisham on 29 October 1971. XR711 never flew again. It was dumped

BELOW
Lavish black/yellow markings began to appear when No 111 Sqn received its F.3s in December 1964. XP738/'G' was scrapped at Wattisham in 1974

TOP
Lightning F.6 (XR747/'X'), one of only two aircraft of this Lightning mark operated by No 111 Sqn, landing at Akrotiri. Fin has sweptback national marking, and three black sea axes on a yellow cross over two red crossed swords highlighted by a black disc

Lightning F.3s XP740/'B' and XR750/'N' ready for the cutting-torch at Wattisham in 1974

Second-line Units

Air Fighting Development Squadron (AFDS)

On 1 September 1959 the Lightning side of the AFDS, under the command of Wg Cdr 'Jimmy' Dell, moved from West Raynham to Coltishall, where extensive alterations had been made in preparation for the supersonic Lightning. The AFDS was part of the Central Fighter Establishment (CFE) which was housed at Tangmere until it moved to West Raynham just after World War II. However, the runway at West Raynham was not suitable for the Lightning.

In December 1959 three DB aircraft, XG334, 335 and 336 were issued to the AFDS at Coltishall. On 5 March 1960, XG334/'A' suffered a hydraulic failure and crashed near Wells-next-the-Sea. Two months later four F.1s arrived to bring the unit's strength up to six and that same month the AFDS Lightnings took part in the annual air defence exercise 'Yeoman', while on detachment to Leconfield.

In October 1962 the CFE and its associated AFDS moved to Binbrook, where it was housed as a lodger unit. The following month it received the first Lightning F.2, XN771. Three more then followed, XN726, 729 and 777. But the latter had a very short career for on 21 December 1962, it overshot the runway at Binbrook. The unfortunate pilot, Air Cmdr Millington, commander of CFE, escaped injury. It was rumoured that the aircraft landed with the auto-throttle engaged and consequently hurtled down the runway at 170 knots (314 km/h) before crashing into the field; the engines flamed out when they became choked with mud. The aircraft, which was then replaced by XN772, sustained heavy damage, but it re-emerged no less than seven years later as an F.2A.

On 1 January 1964, XP695 arrived at Binbrook from Watton for the AFDS. This was the first Lightning F.3 to enter RAF service. The AFDS received three more F.3s but within a few months two had departed. XP695 remained until July, when it was then flown to No 60 MU.

The AFDS did not have a unit insignia, so their aircraft carried a squadron badge on the fin next to the code letter. The name of the unit was stencilled beneath the insignia and a red and black band applied on either side of the nose roundel.

The AFDS was a self-supporting unit responsible for carrying out tactical and operational trials of all new fighter aircraft types and investigating all equipment and aircraft systems. The unit consisted of a Wg Cdr, who was 'Boss', a Sqn Ldr, senior pilot and five other pilots including an American and a Canadian on exchange, plus engineers and ground crew to support the aircraft. The original pilots in the AFDS were 'Ken' Goodwin, Paul Hobley and Peter Collins.

In August 1964, Flt Lt Norman Want (now Wg Cdr) was posted in to the AFDS from No 19 Sqn at Leconfield and at the time of his arrival the unit had on strength two Lightning F.2s, two F.3s and two Hunters for target facilities. The CO at that time was Wg Cdr John Rogers (now Air Marshal).

Flt Lt Want, who was then joined by Flt Lt Ken Hayr, found the work very demanding and just the same as test flying. His first task was flying the F.3 with the Red Top weapons pack.

Flt Lt Want explains about the time he came across his namesake—and that fuel was always a problem with the Lightning: 'The only other time that I ever met anyone with the same name occurred on this particular sortie that we were flying out of here (Binbrook), another front hemisphere Red Top trial which involved various target and fighter speeds. We were running fighters at Mach 1.3, 1.5 and 1.7 and targets similarly 0.2 increment mark down, and running head-on profiles to check parameters of the missiles and weapons system. I remember this particular day I had arranged to land at Coltishall, for we were going to be desperately short of fuel. I was simulating a Mach 1.7 fighter against a 1.5 target. I took off from Binbrook, flew north and then ran south. The target would do the reverse. I had been told I was going to No 74 Sqn, and when I landed at Coltishall to refuel, my boss designate, Wg Cdr 'Ken' Goodwin, came to meet me. But I was a bit harassed because I was trying to make sure that whatever they did with this damn aeroplane, apart from put fuel and oil in it, they didn't touch any of the recordings or the cameras.

'This little airman pitched up with his greasy overalls and said that he was from the photographic section and had come for these things. I was more interested in getting this stuff out than talking to my friend 'Ken' Goodwin and he was really hacked-off, and told me later. I just said 'Hello-goodbye' and he disappeared over the horizon, all miffed. The little airman took the film away to prepare it. When he returned he had a job sheet, as per usual in the Air Force, for me to sign for the work having been completed. I looked at it and saw *my* name written in the column that said tradesman detailed to do the work—J T Want. So I said to this guy 'Cheeky bugger'. 'What, Sir?' 'Look what the've put down here—J T Want to do the work', I protested. 'But that's my name Sir'. Then it all became clear. . .

'We were working on a very fine limit in terms of range and endurance in those days. On another occasion we were doing a front hemisphere trial, running head-on against a high-speed target and I finished up about 80 miles (128 km) northeast of Binbrook, desperately short of fuel, and attempting to get back into Binbrook. We were technically not

Evocative study of two Lightnings: 'DF' (an F.6, nearest the camera) flown by Flt Lt Simon 'Much' Manning, and 'DC' (an F.3) piloted by Sqn Ldr M R Hall

BELOW
Three Lightning F.2s of No 92 Sqn menace the Battle of Britain Memorial Flight's Spitfire Vb, AB910. The markings are typical of the colourful warpaint applied to Lightnings in RAF service during the 1960s. On the right XN735/'N' and in the centre XN783/'A' (BAe)

ABOVE
Lightning T.5 (XS420/'DV') flown by Wg Cdr Norman Want and co-piloted by F/O Andy Holmes launching a Firestreak AAM. Firestreak (originally called 'Blue Jay'), celebrated its 25th anniversary of service in April 1983. Photo taken by Flt Lt Allan from the right hand seat of another T-bird piloted by Flt Lt N R Tuffs. The firing aircraft was manoeuvring hard and only 'welded wing' formation flying made this picture possible

Hot shot: Lightning LFS (light fighter sight) display buried in the wing root of a Lightning F.3 flown by Flt Lt Simon 'Much' Manning. Photo taken by Flt Lt C F Allan sitting in the left hand seat of a T-bird while Flt Lt N R Tuffs did the flying. The engagement was 'set up' by T-bird pilots undergoing the IWI (intercept weapons instructors) course. They asked Much to go into a 1.5G turn, level to port, but Much broke into a 3.5G turn instead. The sight was brought to bear by various hand signals from left hand to right hand seat after turning through 270° (camera prevented mask being worn). The firing range equates to 328 ft (100 m)

*Lightning T.54, 54-651 of the Royal Saudi Air Force
tanks up, previously XM992, the aircraft was later re-
numbered 54-608
(BAe)*

*A 'boomer's' eye view of a Lightning F.3 accepting fuel
from a US Air Force KC-135 tanker*

Lightning F.6 'AF' of No 5 Sqn flown by Flt Lt C T
Lawrence during a practice scramble over RAF Binbrook.
Live Red Tops, guns loaded

BELOW
Lightning F.6, XR773 in yellow primer paint at Binbrook,
May 1981

An unusual sight at Binbrook in September 1975 was this ex-Akrotiri-station flight Lightning T.5, XS452, with a deep pink flamingo on its pink fin, and a pink nose bar. It burst a main wheel tyre on landing

TOP LEFT
Two-tone Lightning F.6 of No 5 Sqn (XR759/'AH') on detachment in RAF Germany

OPPOSITE
Lightning T.5 (XS458/'T') of No 5 Sqn in Cyprus during APC, June 1980. At APC the two Lightning squadrons share their aircraft, and before returning to the UK No 11 Sqn decorated this T-bird with an appropriate message. The white spine helps to reflect heat away from avionics and the Avpin tank

OVERLEAF
Lightning F.6 in full cry

allowed to go supersonic within 30 miles (48 km) of the coast, and the GCI controller, AFDS, was a man called Flt Lt 'Charlie' Fiddler. 'Complete—returning to base'. Back came the reply, 'Check your speed, go the long way round.' 'Negative, I'm going left, the short way round.' So I turned round to come back, decelerating in the turn from Mach 1.5, and got back to Binbrook and landed.

'About 30 minutes later I got this phone call from the Mayor of Bridlington, who was complaining about an aircraft that had dropped a supersonic boom on Bridlington and the surrounding area, and had broken lots of windows in the town. But the thing that really annoyed him was that the sonic boom sounded just like the signal to launch the lifeboat—which was now in the middle of the North Sea. The Mayor was not too impressed with all this. I was very apologetic and did the hot-foot dance routine that most young lads go through when they have been nicked. It was about half a day later that 'Charlie' Fiddler let me off the hook and phoned to tell me that he had been responsible and it really wasn't the Mayor of Bridlington after all'.

Flt Lt Want and Flt Lt 'Ken' Hayr did exchange trials with Americans and French to

TOP
Lightning F.1 (XM137/'F') of the Air Fighting Development Squadron (AFDS) at Coltishall in 1960. This aircraft was later transferred to No 74 Sqn

Lightning F.6 (XR752/'V') operated by the Fighter Command Trials Unit (FCTU) at Binbrook in 1965. The FCTU retained the AFDS nose bars

Two DB Lightnings, XG336/'C' (nearest) and XG335/'B' in service with the AFDS in 1959. XG335 crashed in Wiltshire on 11 January 1965 after starboard gear failed to lower

compare their aircraft and weapons. One aircraft tried was the Mirage and Want found it a very stable aircraft, but underpowered compared to the Lightning. However, the Mirage had greater range and more weapons. In September 1966 Want moved to Leuchars to become a Flight commander with No 74 Sqn for the F.6s coming into service.

The first interim version F.6, XR753, arrived at Binbrook on 16 November 1965 and delivered to the AFDS. It was foliowed a few weeks later by XR752.

On 1 February 1966 the CFE disbanded. The AFDS was renamed the Fighter Command Trials Unit and continued to operate from Binbrook until it disbanded on 30 June 1967. The redundant Lightnings became part of the Binbrook Station Target Facility Flight, with the station's blue lion emblem on the fin.

Target Facility Flights

The concept of supersonic targets for the Lightning squadrons was developed at the Fighter Command Trials Unit (FCTU), Binbrook. Two F.1s were delivered in 1966 (XM164, 22.2.66, and XM137, 15.3.66) and when the FCTU disbanded the Binbrook Target Facility Flight (TFF) was formed.

In April 1966, TFFs were formed at the other Lightning bases, Wattisham and Leuchars. Each

Lightning F.1 (XM137/'Y') of the Binbrook Target Facilities Flight (TFF), with a small 'Binbrook Lion' on the fin

TOP RIGHT
Lightning F.1 XM135 in service with the Leuchars TFF. Note faired-over cannon ports and two lions next to the roundel. XM135 is preserved by the Imperial War Museum at Duxford

OPPOSITE
Lightning F.1 XM139 of the Wattisham TFF sporting sweptback national marking, 'Wattisham Cat' and Union Flag on fin

*Lightning F.1 (XM163/'A') of the Wattisham TFF in
1968. The marking on the fin is an eagle on a galleon.
XM163 was scrapped in December 1974*

unit had three aircraft, two pilots, one engineering officer and 50 groundcrew.

The main task of the TFF was to provide subsonic or supersonic target facilities for the front-line Lightning squadrons. The units could also have been used for local airfield defence, but they did not train for this role, although they did practise air combat manoeuvring (ACM).

The TFF Lightnings at Wattisham each received the name of a cartoon cat, i.e. 'Felix', 'Jinx' and 'Korky' and had yellow/black/yellow nose markings. The Leuchars Lightnings carried a red lion within a yellow flash on either side of the nose roundel. In 1970 the Leuchers TFF was absorbed with No 23 Sqn.

The two other TFFs disbanded, the Binbrook TFF in December 1973, and the two pilots, Flt Lts Nigel Adams and Andy Penswick were posted to 2T squadron at Coltishall. The groundcrews dispersed and the aircraft became decoys.

Lightning F.1 (XM144/'B') of Wattisham TFF taxying at Binbrook. This photograph shows the two types of tail marking—not usually carried on the same aircraft. The 'Wattisham Cat' is above the eagle on a galleon (Grimsby Evening Telegraph)

No 226 Operational Conversion Unit

The first Lightning training unit was the Lightning Conversion Squadron. This unit formed at RAF Middleton St George with Lightning T.4s and the first to arrive was XM970 on 29 June 1962. The LCS was the first RAF unit to be equipped with the T.4 trainer. No markings were applied to the Lightnings, just a tail code. The LCS had an initial strength of ten T.4s and the task of the unit was to convert pilots to the Lightning, aided by flight simulators. The T.4s arrived through the summer and autumn of 1962 and XM993, which was delivered on October 4, ran off the runway on December 12 and was damaged by fire.

Prior to the T.4s, a few single-seat Lightnings from the first three squadrons in Fighter Command so equipped, Nos 56, 74 and 111, had been loaned to the Lightning Conversion Squadron. But these would be only for the day and the aircraft would arrive at Middleton St George early in the morning and after a few hours return to their home base. These were early days while the unit was trying to form as the Lightning became thicker on the ground. In February 1962 one Lightning, XM179 of No 56 Sqn, was detached to Middleton St George for several weeks.

By the spring of 1963 the LCS was fully involved in its comprehensive training task. Most of the instructional staff had previously served with a Lightning squadron or with the Air Fighting Development Squadron.

On 1 June 1963, No 226 Operational Conversion Unit re-formed at Middleton St George from the Lightning Conversion Squadron, at the same time taking over the shadow squadron number and markings of No 145 Sqn, being classified as a reserve front-line unit in time of emergency. By the end of the month the OCU had received the first of its long-awaited Lightning F.1s. These aircraft had previously seen service with No 74 Sqn and after a major overhaul at 60 MU Leconfield XM140, 141, 143, 146, 165 and 167 were delivered to No 226 OCU at Middleton St George. Fins were painted in red and white, and the numerals of the serial applied forward of the nose roundel in large characters.

On 13 April 1964, the OCU moved to Coltishall and a year later the first T.5, XS419, was delivered to the OCU on April 20. The OCU received fifteen of the twenty-two T.5's issued to the RAF.

No 226 OCU was the last unit to receive the F.3, these being XP696, XP737, XR716 and XR718 which arrived at Coltishall from 60 MU in June and July 1970 for use by the OCU's advanced pilots. In May the following year the shadow unit became No 65 Sqn for the F.1/F.1As

Lightning F.1As XM172 and XM182 of No 226 OCU in the markings of No 145 Sqn at RAF Coltishall in the mid-1960s

Box formation of Lightning T.5 trainers of No 226 OCU.
The rear aircraft, XS455, crashed on 6 September 1972

Red Top missiles on Lightning T.5 trainer XS421 of No 226 OCU at Coltishall

TOP LEFT
Lightning F.1A XM189 in a striking red and white scheme used by No 226 OCU at Coltishall

Lightning T.4 trainer XM972 of No 226 OCU

Lightning F.3 XP737 of 2T Sqn, No 226 OCU, on finals
for Binbrook. The fin badge consists of a Latin II
superimposed on a script 'T'. XP737 crashed into the Irish
Sea after a landing gear malfunction on 17 August 1979
when being operated by No 11 Sqn. The pilot, F/O Ray
Knowles, ejected safely

OPPOSITE
Lightning F.1A XM173 on a wet day at Coltishall in the
markings of No 65 Sqn, a 'shadow' unit of No 226 OCU.
The aircraft is marked with eight red chevrons in nose bar
(white background, red border), and a small blue lion on fin

TOP RIGHT
Lightning F.1A XM214 of No 226 OCU (No 65 Sqn
markings) airborne at Cottesmore in 1972

Lightning T.5 XS457 arrived at Binbrook after the rundown of No 226 OCU and became 'C' with No 11 Sqn. This aircraft is currently 'AT' of No 5 Sqn. Picture taken in 1972

and the trainers became No 2T Sqn. The markings for No 65 Sqn consisted of a white bar and four red chevrons either side of the roundel and a blue lion on a white disc on the fin, below the serial number.

As the Jaguar entered service the demands on No 226 OCU lessened as the Lightning pilot training load eased and the unit began to disband. The Lightning F.1As and T.4s of the shadow unit

were withdrawn but the T.5s of No 2T Sqn transferred to Binbrook. Several T.5s were then transferred to 'C' Flight of No 11 Sqn, one being XS457, which arrived on 15 August 1974. The OCU was reactivated and No 226 OCU became the Jaguar Conversion Unit at Lossiemouth in the autumn of 1974.

Lightning Training Flight—LTF

In September 1974 the Lightning Conversion Unit (LCU) formed from 'C' Flight of No 11 Sqn at Binbrook and in October 1975 became the Lightning Training Flight (LTF). The role of this unit was to provide training for the Lightning Squadrons. The LTF has its own engineering personnel, fully combat-capable aircraft but no operational commitments. As a training flight it has no official unit badge but has adopted a version of the blue lion of the station crest to adorn the fins of its aircraft. The LTF operates Lightning F.3s, a T.5 and one F.6. In common with the squadrons the flights aircraft carry either Red Top or Firestreak missiles. For training purposes acquisition rounds are carried which cannot be launched but reproduce every other feature of a live missile and allow pilots to carry out representative sorties up to and including a launch signal. The radar tube picture can be recorded on film and played back during debriefing.

The LTF's single F.6 is always one of the fleet leaders in terms of airframe life and it is used as a target for the student pilots. The aircraft can be fitted with a radar reflector in place of its radar which gives a bigger blip on the student's radar picture. The LTF F.6 also has a non-standard fuel tank in place of the gun pack which gives an additional 100 Imp gal (454 lit) of fuel.

The LTF is the third flying unit at Binbrook. In 1981 there were plans to form a third front-line Lightning squadron at Binbrook, but this was abandoned due to a shortage of airworthy aircraft. In order to keep up to strength the LTF has started courses for ex-Lightning pilots who are now in other postings. This course is known as the 'Lightning Augmentation Force' and the 'LAF' fluorescent diamond badge with LAF in the middle has been applied to some station aircraft. This was an unofficial marking done at senior NCO level.

Note: further reading about the transition of Lightning squadrons into Phantoms can be found in *McDonnell Douglas F-4K and F-4M Phantom II* by Michael Burns, a previous title in the Osprey Air Combat series.

Lightning F.3 (XR716/'D') of the LTF in natural metal finish at Binbrook, early 1970s

TOP LEFT
Lightning T.5 (XV328/'DY') of the Lightning Training Flight (LTF) airborne on dry thrust after a 'roller' landing at Binbrook

OPPOSITE
Tail of Lightning T.4 (XS417/'W') of LTF with fin dominated by 'Binbrook Lion' on 28 July 1977. The beast has dark blue body and yellow/red detail. Significance of Phantom silhouette above 'LTF' not known

BOTTOM LEFT
Two LTF Lightnings: F.3 XP750 (nearest) and T.5 XS458 in a trial grey scheme on finals over RAF Coningsby, 29 April 1976

BELOW
Lightning F.3 XP750 (see page 136) of the 'Lightning Augmentation Force' (LAF), identified by red day-glo star on fin. The red LTF nose bar is retained. Aircraft photographed during a Taceval at Binbrook, 18 February 1980

TOP
Another view of T.5 XS458 (see page 136) in experimental grey camouflage. 'Binbrook Lion' on fin with code letter 'Z'

Lightning F.6 (XR726/'DF') in two-tone grey camouflage with muted 'pink and lilac' national markings at Binbrook, 6 March 1983. Serial and code letters white and 'toned-down' LTF insignia on fin—dark blue lion on white background flanked by red bars

Chapter 3
Lightning Weaponry

The Lightning was first introduced as a quick-reaction, rapid climb-kill and recover aircraft. As an interceptor fuel consumption was a secondary issue when compared to the need to scramble against a high-level threat, for seconds always count in interception missions. To complete the role of the interceptor the Lightning was fitted with radar and two missiles and some were fitted with guns.

During the 60's and early 70's the bulk of Lightning training in the UK was done at high level with the German squadrons concentrating on the low level threat of enemy aircraft. The Lightning therefore had two basic missions: flying under radar control over the sea at heights between sea level and 60,000 ft (18,288 m) and operating autonomously but *visually* at low level over land on designated CAPs (Combat Air Patrols).

The radar, which is controlled by the pilots hand controller in the cockpit, is an I-band unit operating between 8500–9000 Hz. The scanner is housed in the nose of the aircraft and the display is shown to the pilot on a B scope or cathode ray

Red Top (foreground) and Firestreak AAMs shown on two Lightnings for comparison. Red Top is a far more capable weapon, effective against manoeuvring targets in a 'collision-course' attack
(BAe D)

TOP LEFT
*Frying tonight: DB Lightning XG313 ripple-firing 48 ×
2 inch rockets from the ventral weapons pack. XG313 was
scrapped in 1972
(BAe)*

OPPOSITE
*Ventral weapons pack of Lightning F.53 equipped with 48
× 2 inch rockets in retractable launchers
(BAe)*

*Lightning F.53 showing overwing tank, 1,000 lb (454 kg)
bomb, open rocket launcher in ventral pack, and bulged
main wheel door
(BAe)*

tube in the cockpit. The radar scans a sector of sky ahead of the aircraft out to a maximum of 80 nm (148 km). By pressing a small trigger twice on the control stick a lock-on can be achieved against the best target. Three range scales are available—0–10 nm (18 km), 0–40 nm (74 km) and 40–80 nm (74–148 km). The latter is used mainly in coastline painting (i.e. as a navigational aid for recovering to Binbrook when operating over the North Sea). The radar has three modes: Search, Acquisition and Track. The average detection range for a bomber target at high-level is 35–40 nm (64–74 km), a smaller target such as a Lightning itself would not be seen much in excess of 20–25 nm (37–46 km). One weakness with the AI.23 radar is that it suffers from erroneous returns (known as crud) e.g. cloud, sea, land, shipping etc. Fortunately not

Lightning F.53 displaying armament options: Matra 155 rocket launchers and ventral rocket pack (fitted to aircraft), two Red Tops with reconnaissance pack, two Firestreaks, two 1,000 lb (454 kg) bombs, two 30 mm Aden cannons with ammunition, and 68 mm SNEB rockets (BAe)

TOP RIGHT
Twin Matra 155 launchers with a total of 36 SNEB 68 mm rockets. Good detail of starboard main gear, jointly designed by English Electric and Messier. Lightning F.53 (BAe)

all Soviet aircraft are suited to low-level operations.

The attack can range from the classic stern attack (pursuit course) to a head-on attack against a supersonic target. In the latter case the target must be seen by the missile in order for the engagement to be completed, aiming to get between $1.50°$ and $1.80°$ angle-off. The attack preferred by the Lightning pilot is the stern attack because it gives him the option of using missiles or guns. The pilot aims to get between two and four miles astern to carry out his attack. The battle tactics for the Lightning pilot still stress the use of the Mk 1 eyeball. The Lightning pilot can lock on to his target, but there are penalties for doing so. Firstly, the majority of Soviet aircraft have an ESM capability and a lock-on gives away any

chance of surprise. The target can jam the attacker's radar or pinpoint the direction of the attack and take the necessary evasive action—or both. So the Lightning pilots carry out their attacks in search mode using a relatively new modification which allows the missiles to be fired without locking on. This method of attack demands more of the pilot, but it does not alert the enemies RWR (radar warning receiver) to the specific threat of imminent attack.

It takes up to eighteen months for Lightning pilots to become fully assimilated with the radar, but this experience is not easily lost. By understanding the radar display a pilot can assess target height, heading and speed. In a very short time it gives the Lightning pilot a great advantage in air combat, because he can avoid alerting enemy

aircraft that he is in killing distance. To calculate heading and height of target aircraft the Lightning pilot carries around in his head a conglomeration of figures which are readily available. E.g. target at 20 nm (37 km), 10° left is 3.3 nm (6.1 km) displaced. Target at 10° elevation and 15 nm (27 km) is 15,000 ft (4,572 m) above.

The Lightning is the poor relation regarding ECM, for money has never been made available to fit suitable equipment. The Lightning pilots therefore get airborne without the basic equipment thought necessary by NATO to survive an all-out air war.

The two 30 mm Aden guns carry a total of 120 rounds per gun and fire at the rate of 1,200 rounds per minute, giving a six second burst. A two-second burst could do a lot of damage if the aircraft is in range. The guns are harmonized for 450 yards (411 m), which is fine until taking into account that many Soviet bombers have defensive guns which have a lethal range out to 1,000 yards (914 m) or so. This is nothing new, the Germans had the same problem against the Fortresses in World War II.

The Lightning is cleared to carry Firestreak or Red Top missiles. Red Top missiles are cleared for flight with or without Luneberg lenses. Red Top is a second generation air-to-air missile,

Loading 30 mm rounds into the ammo tank of a Lightning F.6. Grease is smeared around the gun barrel exit and shockwave deflectors (extreme left), to protect the rear-bodies of the missiles from blast damage

developed out of the experience gained with Firestreak and incorporating many of the scientific improvements in missile technology which came about during Firestreak development.

The Red Top can be launched head on against a high-speed target or against a medium-fast target, from 30° stern sector if manoeuvring.

The basic design concept of Firestreak has been proved sound by rigorous testing and extensive trials under service conditions. Red Top, therefore, retains the configuration of four fixed wings and four moving rear control surfaces, with the design being further optimized to give operation over a very wide altitude and speed range. The infrared guidance system has been further developed to allow target interception from virtually any direction. However, the missile zone is limited as the missile needs to be launched aiming well ahead of target. The missile can be fired up to 55,000 ft (16,764 m) and will snap up a further 10,000 ft (3,048 m). It accelerates to Mach 1.7 above fighter speed and it can be fired from as low as 300 ft (91 m).

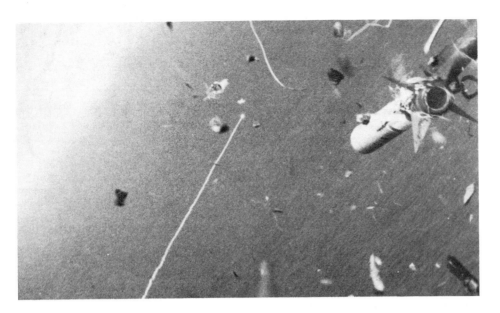

Red Top AAM breaking up immediately after launch. The missile was fired from low level over the Irish Sea at the target visible in the centre of these pictures, a Jindivik drone towing a flare. The Lightning ingested the debris, sustaining category 2 damage; both engines had to be changed and the tail was also hit. High-speed film in the camera gun recorded this sequence. The Lightning's pitot head tube is descernible in the foreground

1983 was the 25th anniversary of the Firestreak missile. It has seen sterling service worldwide, though it has never had to be fired in anger. Although an old missile by today's standards both Firestreak and its younger brother, Red Top, are very capable and have tremendous terminal lethality; such that detonation within 20 yards (18 m) of an enemy aircraft would probably destroy it. However, it must be stressed that both Red Top and Firestreak require massive *in situ* support from the aircraft; namely a large weapons pack for cooling, heating, hydraulics and electrics—unlike modern missiles, e.g. Sidewinder, which require very little in the way of on-board support and next to no maintenance. The big drawback is only two AAMs and this is one of the Lightning's weaknesses.

The export Lightnings had more weaponry hardware and the armament mix possibilities included Red Top or Firestreak missile pack; 48 2 inch rockets carried in the fuselage forward weapon bay, 1,000 lb (454 kg) bombs, Matra rocket launchers and Aden cannon. A reconnaissance pack was also available.

Obviously money was the reason why the RAF Lightnings were not armed like the export versions. Even in its twilight years the Lightning could be given more bite if fitted with a couple of Sidewinder missiles.

Lightning F.3 (XP706/'BM') of No 11 Sqn at RAF Valley in 1982 fitted with a pair of AIM-9L Sidewinder drill rounds. This is definitely a non-operational configuration . . .

Chapter 4 A Comparison with the F-106

Wg Cdr 'Mike' Streten, aged 40, joined the London University Air Squadron in 1962 and learned to fly on Chipmunks. He joined the RAF in 1963 and his training was undertaken on Jet Provosts at RAF Leeming, where he was awarded his wings in 1966. He was then posted to No 4 FTS at RAF Valley, where he flew the Gnat. In August 1968 he moved to Chivenor on the Hunter pre-Lightning course and flew the Lightning F.1 and F.3 with No 226 OCU at Coltishall and in July 1968 joined No 23 Sqn at Leuchars.

After a tour with No 23 Sqn he moved back to Coltishall flying Lightnings with 2T, 226 OCU. On his second tour he was flight commander and chief weapon instructor. From July 1972 to May 1975 he flew F-106s in America at Tyndall Air Force Base, Florida. Upon his return to the UK he spent some time at MoD and Staff College. He took a jet refresher course at Leeming on Jet Provosts and then was posted to No 4 FTS, Valley, flying Hunter T.7s. In December 1978 he moved to No 5 Sqn at RAF Binbrook, flying Lightnings, and was appointed to command the squadron in July 1982. He enjoys watching and flying the Lightning, having flown the Mark F.1, F.1A, F.3, T.4, T.5 and F.6. To date he has flown over 1,600 hours on Lightnings. Wg Cdr Streten still flies about sixteen hours a month, which could be twenty-two sorties—and still finds time for his paper work. He is married with two daughters and for relaxation enjoys shooting and painting.

During his stay at Tyndall Air Force Base he flew the F-106 Delta Dart single-seat all-weather interceptor fighter and being an experienced Lightning pilot compares the two aircraft.

'During the period from August 1972 to May 1975 I was fortunate enough to be posted on an exchange tour with the then Air Defense Command (ADC) of the United States Air Force based at Tyndall Air Force Base, Panama City, Florida. The unit on which I served was the Interceptor Weapons School as a qualified weapons instructor on the staff. Our flying syllabus was such that all aspects of air interceptor tactics, using the F-106 Delta Dart, were explored in depth.

'To someone who had flown the Lightning, which in comparison to the '106 is a high performance but unsophisticated interceptor, the Delta Dart represented a major step forward in the concept of an integrated air defence system, combining intimately ground based radar systems with computer processing linked to airborne fighters equipped with modern digital computers and the whole system communicating by datalink. In its concept the F-106 was a bold step forward in the use of technology. It was for many years the longest-ranged fighter in the world with its standard fit of two wing tanks and full internal armament load. The aircraft could fly 1,500 mile (2,413 km) legs easily and mission times of $2\frac{1}{2}$ hours were normal for this aircraft. In comparing the aircraft to the Lightning the following areas should be considered. Firstly airframe performance. In simple terms the Lightning is capable of a climb to 36,000 ft (10,975 m) 15 miles (24 km) from its base in full afterburner and to the same height by 30 miles (48 km) in military power. On the other hand the figures for the F-106 were 65 and 128 miles (104 and 205 km). So compared to the Lightning the F-106 seemed underpowered. On the other hand acceleration to Mach 2 in the Lightning can be achieved relatively quickly but not sustained for long due to its poor endurance. The F-106 with its greater fuel load achieved high Mach figures more slowly, but could sustain them for far longer.

Wg Cdr 'Mike' Streten (minus moustache) in Lightning cockpit

'In air combat manoeuvring the Dart had the advantage of being the lowest wing-loaded fighter in the world and was highly manoeuvrable and light on the controls, but was disadvantaged by the high induced drag caused by a conventional delta at high angles of attack. The Lightning has no vices whatever and gives any switched-on pilot plenty of warning that departure from controlled flight is imminent. However, in certain areas of flight the F-106 could depart rapidly and was not necessarily recoverable. An interesting footnote to this is that there was an aircraft at Tyndall that had been abandoned by its pilot when the aircraft got into a spin. The aircraft somehow managed to land on a snow bank in the full view of a local sheriff, who observed the aircraft come to a halt with engine running but—to his horror—no pilot in the cockpit. The aircraft was effectively undamaged, subsequently recovered and restored to flying condition.

'In concert with a consideration of performance the cockpit operating areas can be reasonably compared. The Lightning cockpit is, by my reckoning, the smallest and most compact in the world—whereas the F-106 has a large, comfortable American style of cockpit with all the operating

. . . 'give me the Lightning any day of the week'. Wg Cdr 'Mike' Streten at the controls of Lightning F.6 XS899/'AA' on a low level sortie north of the Humber. No 5 Sqn insignia, green maple leaf in middle of red bars, on fin

TOP RIGHT
Convair F-106 Delta Dart of the 318th Fighter Interceptor Squadron launches a ATR-2A Genie AAM from its weapons bay. Operational version (AIR-2A) armed with nuclear warhead
(US Air Force via Robert F Dorr)

RIGHT
Streten: . . . 'the Lightning is capable of a climb to 36,000 ft (10,975 m) 15 miles (24 km) from its base in full afterburner and to the same height by 30 miles (48 km) in military power. . . . the figures for the F-106 were 65 miles (104 km) and 128 (205)'. F-106A-105-CO, 59-27, of the 171st Fighter Interceptor Squadron, 191st Fighter Interceptor Group (ADC), of the Michigan Air National Guard at Selfridge ANGB, 1976
(Mich ANG via Robert F Dorr)

switches easily accessible and—perhaps more to the point—in view. The lookout from both aircraft is very similar, although the F-106 had been improved by introducing a clear canopy giving a much better view upwards. The unique windscreen design of both the F-102 and F-106 was no problem to the pilot because a so-called vision splitter enabled the pilot to look through the two screens as if they were one.

'On the subject of airframe performance the 1975 version of the aircraft had the finest electrical redundancy system I have ever seen on a single-seat aircraft. A double power failure was required before the pilot had any concerns whatsoever. Unlike the Lightning, which has hydraulic power to its brakes, the F-106 uses high-pressure air for braking and operation of its weapon bay and launch rails from a ground-charged reservoir. However, the use of nose wheel steering and a switch, operable in the ground situation only, which opened the engine nozzle to the fully open position, made the aircraft easy to handle on the ground with little use of brake. The big disadvantage however was that there was no parking brake and this was definitely a problem if a long delay in departure clearance occurred at the take-off point when the outside air temperature was 95°F (35°C) or better with high humidity, the greenhouse effect being most pronounced. Engine control was different in the F-106 because the J79 engine, being multispooled, did not respond to the RPM gauge in the instantaneous fashion that the Lightning pilot is accustomed to.

The operable gauges for F-106 engine operation were normally the fuel-flow gauge, which did not register the increased flow with the afterburner operating, and the engine pressure ratio (EPR) gauge. By consulting a set of tables, EPR values were calculated for take-off and gave a direct value equating to engine thrust at take-off or cruise. Thus RPM and turbine temperature were effectively irrelevant—you either had the thrust and went, or the EPR was not achieved and there was obviously something wrong with the engine.

'For its generation the Hughes Aircraft MA-1 radar and computer system of the '106 represented the apogee of 1960s pulse-doppler radar technology. The radar had many and various modes to enable it to lock on to and then hold lock against a whole variety of electronic counter measures, this coupled with the fact that the radar was fully integrated with an infrared search and tracking system that enabled radar target tracking with IR back-up or vice versa. The aircraft computer system was programmed via datalink to either the SAGE (strategic air/ground environment) or BUIC (back-up interceptor control) so that ground control could send command signals to an individual aircraft and operate various instruments within the cockpit to command the pilot, or the aircraft itself if in autopilot mode. In the latter case all the pilot was required to do was accelerate the aircraft to the commanded speed, lock up to the target and squeeze the fire committal switch—the aircraft did the rest. The interceptor and target positions were shown moving over a fixed map display on the so-called tactical situation display (TSD). The TSD held something like 26 maps covering the whole continental USA and from any position one could select a destination in navigation mode and the aircraft would fly there on autopilot. The MA-1 navigation system utilized a first-generation inertial platform updated by Tacan and was an accurate system in this mode. If Tacan was not available the platform and computer dead reckoned, but without the benefit of any wind calculation.

'The whole weapon-system was completed by the weapon fit held internally in a pneumatically operated weapons bay. The F-106 carried the AIR 2A Genie ballistic rocket with a small atomic warhead and two pairs of either AIM-4F (semi-active) or AIM-4G (IR) missiles. The normal fit being 2 × AIM-4F and 2 AIM-4G. The missiles were in fact guided 'hittiles' and always fired in pairs, although the pilot selected whether one or two pairs were to be fired. The Genie was considered to be the ultimate air-to-air weapon and its ballistic nature explains why so much care was taken with the radar's ability to hold and maintain lock. Clearly the F-106, even with this brief resume of its capabilities, was impressive by any standards, but on balance give me the Lightning any day of the week.'

Chapter 5
Binbrook Lightnings

The role of the Binbrook Lightnings is fourfold—
1) The policing of UK air space in peacetime.
2) To defend the UK in time of emergency.
3) The air defence of the Royal Navy at sea in NATO water.
4) Overseas deployment, now sadly diminished in recent years.

Royal Air Force Binbrook still plays a significant role in the air defence of the United Kingdom, as a major station within No 11 Group Strike Command. Binbrook has been a Lightning station since 1965 when No 5 Sqn re-formed. With the arrival of No 11 Sqn in 1972, Binbrook became an all-Lightning station.

Binbrook's Nos 5 and 11 Sqns are the last two front-line units in the Royal Air Force to operate the Lightning. Sharing the base at Binbrook is the Lightning Training Flight (LTF) operating with the F.3 and F.6 fighter version plus the T.5 fully operational two-seat trainer.

Within the LTF is the Lightning Augmentation Force (LAF) which was established to provide extra operational front-line aircraft during exercise periods and in times of emergency.

On 3 August 1979 celebrations were held at RAF Binbrook to mark the 25th anniversary of the only all-British supersonic aircraft to enter full-scale squadron service. The highlight of the special

Lightning F.3 (XR713/'AR') of No 5 Sqn on the flight line at Binbrook in 1983. Live Firestreak 'acquisition round' to starboard, balanced by a dummy opposite. The F.3 has since been withdrawn from squadron service

display was the anniversary line-up of seven specially marked Lightnings in the markings of Nos 19, 23, 56, 74, 92 and 111 Sqns, which had previously been equipped with Lightnings.

With the ageing Lightning having to soldier on into the 1980s Binbrook's alert has now been reduced to approximately two weeks in five on call. The 'Southern Q' duty is rotated between Binbrook, Wattisham and Coningsby. The two Lightnings in the 'Q-shed' are maintained in a fully-armed state with live missiles and loaded

Fighter pilot: Flt Lt 'Chris' Allan was awarded his wings at RAF Valley in 1978. He was the last RAF student to qualify on the Gnat. Now serving with the LTF, Flt Lt Allan was responsible for many of the air-to-air shots found in this book

BELOW
Lightning F.3 XP748—the gate guardian at RAF Binbrook. No 5 Sqn insignia visible, No 11 Sqn markings on the other side. When the aircraft was repainted in 1983 the markings were changed over

BOTTOM RIGHT
Lightning F.6 (XR747/'BF') of No 11 Sqn at Binbrook, 28 August 1982. XR747 was previously operated by No 5 Sqn, red nose bars not removed since it emerged from storage

cannons, fully fuelled and ready to go at a moment's notice.

The Binbrook Lightnings keep tabs on the Russian surveillance aircraft, either Tu-95 *Bears*, Tu-16 *Badgers*, M-4 *Bisons* or Il-18 *Coots* which are regularly intercepted many hundreds of miles off the coast of the United Kingdom. The Soviet Air Force and Navy aircraft track around the North Cape and down towards the British Isles and the Atlantic. To the Binbrook pilots it is a case of cops and robbers over the North Sea.

Until the air-defence version of the Tornado comes into service the exceptional skill and dedication of the ground crews are needed to keep the ageing Lightning flying and that special breed of men to fly them. There are about a dozen pilots with over 2,000 hours on the Lightning, the highest being Sqn Ldr 'Dave' Carden with over 3,000 hours, followed by Flt Lt 'Jim' Wild and Flt Lt 'Chris' Stevens, both with over 2,500 hours. Binbrook will always be known as the home of the Lightning.

To give some idea of what is expected from both men and machines, fly with Sqn Ldr 'Dave' Carden of No 5 Sqn on a routine CAP exercise....

'A fine summer's morning, all in for met brief and for once he gets it right—clear skies, light winds, 25 mile (40 km) visibility—a great day for anything. Check the flying programme in the squadron's ops room; good news I'm leading a four-ship for a low-level CAPEX with in-flight refuelling support. I wonder who the opposition will be today?—ye gods, ten pairs of Jaguars in waves of two and four at one minute intervals, all hell bent on reaching their targets and dead keen to have a go at an air defence fighter on the way. Better check the team I have with me very carefully—yes, no problem there, everyone low-level evasion cleared and all operational—this will really work us out. Better start to decide the tactical plan as there are going to be some critical moments during this mission.

'Firstly the CAPEX over the sea. Must be near enough to the tanker towline to reach it without burning much gas as we are going to be desperately short. Next, it has to be across the Jags track and in a position where we can 'paint' the coastline on the radar occasionally. We'll pick the height to fly when we get there and see the haze layer depth, and where will the sun be at that time of the morning?—that just might be important! Now the tanker. No problems there as we practise almost daily, but must make sure we leave low level with the fuel to join up with it and there are four of us to refuel, so it's going to take a correspondingly longer time. Finally, the overland part of the sortie. We have to protect an area that the Jags are going to attack. A much more difficult prospect, so check the maps for towns, pylons, danger areas, study the terrain and imagine I am

the Jag leader—where will he run in to the target? What IP (initial point) to target feature will he use? How will he fly his formations?

'I eventually pick 2 CAPs as possibilities, but I am prepared to modify them in the light of the conditions at the time. Brief up the formation covering the minutiae of detail it is necessary to discuss when operating in a complicated engagement zone. Stress the really important details. "Remember, cross cover is vital at all stages of the sortie including on the tanker, any singleton will be picked off quickly. If you engage then always do so as a covering pair and never commit both aircraft into a fight at the same time. Keep a careful check of fuel and position and beware of target fixation when staring at an enemy in the gunsight." This last problem can creep up when the adrenalin is flowing, and jet wash can do violent things to your aircraft, especially at low-level. Finally the vital points—"Keep covering and keep it simple!"

'Out we go, aircraft all ready, groundcrew in position, air traffic control poised to assist. "Maple check in". "Maple 2,3,4" they reply. "Start GO". Everything turns and burns as advertised by BAC and Rolls-Royce. We taxy out to the end of the runway, and when cleared by ATC, line up in pairs for take-off. With the power at 85% per engine I receive a thumbs up from three other cockpits and with a nod of my head the No 2 and

I roll. A quick check on the No 2 to see him still tucked in with me, another nod and we select reheat. They light with a great bang and we accelerate rapidly to 175 knots (324 km/h). We lift away still glued together. Gear up, flaps up and a final nod to cancel the reheat selection. Nos 3 and 4 rolling 10 seconds behind us and at 350 knots (628 km/h) we form up in battle formation. For the Lightning this is 3,000 yards (2,700 m), between pairs with the wingmen 60° swept back from his leader and on the outsides of the formation. Already the heads are swivelling as we check and recheck the security of the formation and we hurtle out at low-level to the operating area. Check the radar, weapons, aircraft systems, fuel position and all the time the integrity of the formation—we are fair game for anybody to have a sniff at us flying in this sort of formation. No 4 is straggling a little (No 4s always tend to straggle) so I snap at him to keep in position and we settle into our defensive posture.

'On CAP now and the conditions are ideal. I split the team into its pairs to go to individual CAPs, close enough to render assistance to one another if necessary, but far enough apart to cover the Jaguars' penetration front. No radio calls now as we concentrate on holding CAP and swivelling our heads around. I begin to sweat with the concentration; have we missed them? Are they even now manoeuvring to bounce us? Come on,

Lightning F.6 (XR726/'F') of the LAF at Binbrook, 26 May 1982. Two-tone Barley grey scheme with 'pink and lilac' national markings and white serial. Small LAF badge above code letter on fin, both day-glo red

OPPOSITE
Lightning F.6 XR759 with LAF badge repeated on overwing tanks at Binbrook, 14 May 1982

come on, where are they? A sleek, grey shark-like shape flickers into the edge of my vision, very low over the sea and almost merged with it. "Maple lead bogies 2 o'clock crossing right/left, low, range 4 miles, Maple 2 buster GO, bogies heading north now 12 o'clock to us". Maple 2 calls contact, "Maple 3,4 bogies approaching your CAP in 30 secs." I call we are turning onto their track and accelerating at a furious rate. "Maple 2 cover me high and check for trailing aircraft." I'm in for a sneaky kill before they see us, and low over the sea at 480 knots (888 km/h) I close to missile range on the left-hand man. Sight on quickly now and the missile 'sees' his infrared-hot jet pipe. Pull the trigger and the camera runs, capturing it all for posterity—"Fox 2 on the left man reversing to starboard." Damn they have seen us and are breaking starboard at 6G. I close rapidly on the right-hand man as I cut the corner and reheat in

and slide into range—can I get him before his
wingman gets me. Too much angle-off for the
missile now and I select guns and concentrate on
the gunsight. My number 2 calls the other Jag out
of range and I pull the sight on to my man at 400
yards (365 m). He is fully aware of what is taking
place and as the nose of my aircraft sniffs at him
he begins to manoeuvre violently—pull right,
bunt, kink, reverse, pull left, bunt, jink—and in
and out of his slipstream I jerk with the sea 250 ft
(76 m) below us as we turn, sweat and curse. Hold
the sight on, where's my No 2, check the fuel,
watch the sea, where's his No 2, reverse the turn,
watch the G, hold the sight on. I fire four or five
half-second bursts of the cameragun at him and
break hard away out of the tortuous circle. There's
my No 2 still covering and he reports a missile
shot on the other Jag as it tried to turn in on me.
3 and 4 are calling their engagement with 4 Jags

*Lightning F.3 XR716 of 2T Sqn, No 226 OCU, adds a
bit of drama to Binbrook's first open day as station firemen
hose down the aircraft after a fuel leak*

and we race to assist them. "Knock-it-off," calls
number 3, "they're running out heading north."
    'I check the fuel across the formation and decide
we have just enough to join up before going on to
the tanker. "Maple RV at Flamborough Head
5,000 ft (1,524 m)", and we quickly pick up our
position again. Now petrol, and as quickly as
possible, so stick hard back and we rocket
skywards at 450 knots (833 km/h). The Lightning
has a phenomenal rate of climb and 30 sec later we
are sitting at 30,000 ft (9,146 m) at 0.9 Mach.
Here comes the tanker dead on cue as always and
we swing into the complicated dance of refuelling

four aircraft. "Maple 3 and 4 cover us at 4 miles" I call, Tango, "Maple 1 and 2 are we clear to join you." "Maple you are clear," he replies. We position for refuelling and from the pods on each wing of the tanker the hoses unwind. Thick, long, black snakes with what looks like a waste paper basket on the end, they hang in the airflow behind the wings inviting us in. We greedily suck in the fuel at 1,000 lb (454 kg) per minute and are soon topped up. We then reverse positions with 3 and 4 and they refuel while we guard the formation from 4 miles (6.4 km) behind. This slick operation taking place 6 miles (9.6 km) up and at 7 miles (11.2 km) a minute is soon complete and leaving the tanker to continue on his philanthropic way we depart to undertake the third part of the sortie.

"'Idle, idle, demist on, airbrakes GO'', and down we dive to low level again aiming for the overland operating area. This time we will operate as a 4 ship altogether on one CAP to bring maximum cover and fire power to bear—it's going to be busy for a while. Down the valleys, over the hills, miss the towns and pylons. Round and round on CAP we go, covering, checking, and the fuel runs steadily away. Calculate fuel remaining to departure, time left on CAP, range from base, time we can stay in a fight at full power, fuel, position, time, fuel. . . . Suddenly through the 6 o'clock of the formation slide the Jags and they have already seen us and are turning in. "Maple hard inwards turnabout go, bogies 6 o'clock. 3 and 4 pull high." My No 2 calls contact four Jags and that he is engaging so I cover him in while 3 and 4 cover us both. The Jags reverse down track and we race after them, twisting, turning, round the hills, down the valleys. With the luxury of two aircraft covering me I am able to engage one of the rear Jags and he goes into his deadly dance again, pull, bunt, jink, reverse. This time it's much more difficult and I only get 2 bursts of cameragun on him before a frantic call from my number 3 changes everything. "Maple 1 and 2 break port," and out we go in a mad climbing turn as 3 and 4 engage the pair who had been sneaking in on us. Round we go with the sweat pouring down and the oxygen mask slipping on our faces under the G. Then blessed relief the Jags reverse off us and disengage. Mentally reminding myself to buy No 3 a beer we roll back down after them. It's easy now and this time the missile 'sees' before they get down to low level and we launch. "Fox 2 and closing guns on the starboard man." The Jag violently reverses but we box him in and he drops down to his base height—a good tactic but the blood is hot and we nail him hard. At 300 yards (274 m) he is filling the gunsight and I press the trigger once more, then it's out of the combat area with 2 covering me and 3 and 4 checking the back door. "Maple reform—check fuel." Maple 4 calls bingo fuel, No 4s always use too much fuel in

combat, and so we ease out of the area. This is the dangerous moment as we don't have enough fuel for any more engagements and might be poorly placed to fight our way out, so we swivel our heads and check down track. The sky is miraculously clear and we lift up for the run into base.

'Back in the circuit and a neat break to show the watching critics just how it should be done and we land in turn. "Maple clear the runway," calls No 4 and we taxy back in to our dispersal pan. Back to normality, car bills, taxes, admin problems, station duty officer, domestic problems and the Boss inquiring why we used so much aircraft fatigue. Is it only 1 hr 15 min since we took off? What an aircraft—what a job.'

Sqn Ldr 'Dave' Carden, aged 44, 'A' Flight Commander No 5 Squadron was educated at Portsmouth Northern Grammar school and joined the Royal Air Force as an RAF apprentice in 1956. His flying training was undertaken at RAF Syerston on Jet Provosts and at RAF Valley on Gnats. He then flew Hunters at Chivenor before being posted to No 226 OCU at Coltishall early in 1966. In February 1967 he was posted to his first Lightning unit, No 74 Sqn at Leuchars, and after three months went to Tengah. In 1969 he transferred to go to Binbrook on No 5 Sqn and also helps run the Lightning Flight Simulator.

After a tour with No 11 Sqn as weapons instructor and a tour with No 19 Sqn in Germany he was back again to Binbrook, where in a short time he was promoted to Sqn Ldr and then posted to MoD. He then came back into flying and re-trained before being posted back to Binbrook early in 1980, becoming 'A' Flight Commander on No 5 Sqn.

With over 3,000 hours on Lightnings—the longest ever—he is 'Mister Lightning'. His second home is the Lightning cockpit and he has flown every version of the Lightning except the F.2. The one he enjoyed flying the most was the F.2A because it was 'operational' and did a good job. Married with two children his hobbies include music, skiing and any sport.

These are the men who are not afraid to take on the odds—even with the ageing Lightning. With sheer, naked aggressiveness they will not back away from the challenge. It is men like these that saved us in the past, and who could save us in the future—if only the mount matched the jockey.

QRA—Quick Reaction Alert

Since 1970, the Lightning F.6 aircraft have been fitted with 30 mm cannon in the belly tanks which are not as final as the missiles if they need to give a warning 'shot across the bows' to stubborn customers. Russian aircraft usually track down off the Norwegian coast around the top of Scotland into the Atlantic—this would put up the Leuchars QRA aircraft. Many times the Russians 'stray' down the North Sea and when they do this puts up the Binbrook Lightnings.

Quick Reaction Alert is the bread and butter existence of the Lightning pilot. It is the primary aim of training to qualify the new pilot for this role. This training involved many sorties of practice intercepts (PIs) against targets simulating any airborne threat. When this basic phase of training is complete pilots are declared limited operational, which qualifies them for Quick Reaction Alert (QRA).

After all the stringent training the first days of holding QRA can be an anticlimax—there are the butterflies of checking out a fully armed aircraft and being at minutes' notice of a scramble as well as the prestige of 'protecting the nation', but after twelve hours of sitting around talking and reading with the likelihood of a scramble diminishing it can be boring and increasingly grows to be a chore with very little 'glamour' involved. Start 0900 hours each day for twenty-four hour period at ten-minute alert. The two pilots coming onto QRA duty change before going to the Q-shed and take with them an overnight bag, i.e. towel, soap, toothbrush. Also, a book and any work for a stint of QRA can be a godsend and lets the pilots catch up with their paperwork and those little jobs that are connected with the day-to-day running of the service.

On handover from off-going pilots the aircraft is checked together with all communications—telephone to station and GPO and telephone to Sector Operations Centre (Ground Control Radar). Once the alarm bells to Air Traffic and groundcrew have been checked it is time for a cup of tea to help unwind the tension that has built up with the knowledge of QRA duty. Once the action starts the ice-cool nerve of these highly trained men will take over—but it is the waiting that brings on the butterflies. While the pilots settle in with a cup of tea and a bite to eat a quick call to the Met Man to check out the weather and then speak to radar controller about 'activity' and the likelihood of a scramble. Some pilots then set up their cockpits to individual preference. Then wait. . . . Too early for television, so chat, do some paperwork or read a book. Check groundcrew are OK and that lunch will be on time. The pilots look forward to the tasty meals which they are not normally used to. These meals are cooked by the groundcrew who live in the Q-shed for up to ten days at a time—more recently specialist cooks have

Sgt Allen and his crew load Flt Lt 'Mike' Chatterton's Lightning F.6 (XR758/'AF') with 30 mm HE ammunition prior to QRA readiness. No 5 Sqn aircraft

OPPOSITE
Flt Lts 'Mike' Chatterton (left) and 'Chris' Allan on QRA duty sit and wait in immersion suits for a scramble that may never come. Note the bed behind the sliding door (left)

been brought in to ease their busy schedule of servicing.

Unmistakeably, the most exciting thing about QRA is the scramble *if* it comes. Some pilots spend a whole career never mind tour (2½ years) without ever seeing a Soviet aircraft. Those that have will never forget it and generally become the permanent Q2 pilot (reserve scramble after Q1) with a second scramble becoming extremely rare.

Sometimes there can be hours' notice of a scramble, but occasionally one may be scrambled from bed. The need to become a quick change artist becomes obvious with only minutes to dress, strap into the aircraft and get airborne.

As the alarm bells sound the pilots dress, don Bone Dome (helmet) and Mae West (life jacket). As the pilots get ready the groundcrew rush out to connect ground power and open doors.

There are lots of checks to do on strap-in and

start-up and once done scramble instructions are given. Canopy closed and seat pins out, making seat live. The adrenalin runs high as the ageing angel roars down the runway and pulls effortlessly into the night sky.

Getting airborne is just the start of a long chain of decision-making events. The Lightning was not designed for long transit and patrol sorties and therefore requires air-to-air refuelling (AAR).

Once take-off checks are complete the aircraft is vectored towards the tanker rendezvous. After joining up with the tanker the Lightning and tanker will remain together until the intercept area is reached. This may involve a transit of hundreds of miles with several 'plugs' (into the tanker). During the transit the pilot will confirm diversion airfield weather including overseas airfields should Britain 'sock in' with low cloud and strong winds rendering airfields unusable.

Following the instructions of the fighter controller, the Lightning will leave the tanker to intercept the intruder, but care is taken not to lose track of the tanker's position as it will supply the fuel for the long transit home.

As the Lightning turns away from the tanker the pilot will detect the unknown target on his own radar—up to that point he has been controlled by ground radar, and using the techniques taught

*Lightning F.6 taxies out of the Q-shed. The protective
rubber caps over the Red Tops have been removed*

over the many months of training, will pull alongside the unknown aircraft and show his presence. According to international rules and procedures this will be on the port side—in sight of the target's crew. Normally the Soviet crew will acknowledge the intercept, but unless it enters friendly air space nothing more can be done to restrict its movements.

Having shown fighter presence the Lightning pilot then works against time to photograph the target aircraft before the need to return to the tanker. The Lightning must always have enough fuel to recover to the nearest suitable diversion airfield should there be a malfunction with the air-to-air refuelling system.

OPPOSITE
Lightning F.6 tailing a Tupolev Tu-142 Bear-F used for maritime reconnaissance by the Soviet Navy

F.6 formation take-off by XR754/'AE' (left) and XR761/'AC' of No 5 Sqn. Pairs take-off only permitted if the two Lightnings are of the same mark. Using reheat on take-off is standard procedure for F.6, but F.3 can manage on military power

On one occasion Flt Lt Allan intercepted a *Bear* about 1,000 miles (1,600 km) north of Binbrook. The *Bear* is a very big aircraft and therefore because of its wing area can fly more slowly at a given altitude. This can make the taking of photographs very difficult, for the pilot must use a hand held camera—and flying close to the stalling speed of the Lightning he must take care not to mishandle the aircraft and also operate safely when flying so close to another aircraft which might be only a matter of feet away. Even in daylight this can be very difficult and at night demands a lot of skill and ice cool nerves with split-second judgement. This does highlight the need for two man crews.

Relationships between Lightning pilots and the crews of Russian reconnaissance bombers are usually all smiles and waves, with each taking photographs of each other. Having completed the photographs and a respectful wave of acknowledgement between aircraft crews the Lightning must recover to base and as he swings for home his first thought is fuel and the tanker—after all the tanker too must have enough fuel to

get back to base.

Concentration must not fail on the return flight as there are still decisions to be made, not to mention the ever-present risk of an aircraft emergency and there is still a long way to go. It is very reassuring for the pilots to see the friendly shores of a familiar coastline having operated over the cold seas to the north.

After landing there are reports to write and the Lightning to be 'turned round' ready for another scramble. When this done the pilot will start to unwind and settle down to a nice cup of tea and perhaps something to eat—he may have been airborne several hours—one sortie took 5½ hours.

OPPOSITE
Two-tone grey Lightning F.6 (XS936/'DF'), in company with the more conventionally camouflaged F.3 (XP753/'DC') which fired a Firestreak on this sortie. On a later flight, 'DC' crashed into the sea near Scarborough on 26 August 1983, killing the pilot, Flt Lt 'Mike' Thompson

BELOW LEFT AND BELOW
Where's the f . . . ing ladder? F/O Wyatt trying to avoid a giant leap for mankind from Lightning F.6 (XR757/'BE') of No 11 Sqn at Binbrook on 18 May 1983. A balancing act between in-flight refuelling probe and Red Top put him safely on the concrete

Ejection. . .

The Lightning version with the best accident record per number of type in service was the F.2/F.2A with only three losses out of 39 F.2's used by the Royal Air Force (five converted to F.52's). It will also be seen that 1969 was the best year for Lightning losses. Only one aircraft was written-off out of nine operational squadrons, an OCU and three TFFs.

In the early 1970s the Lightning had a crash record almost on a par with the notorious F-104 Starfighter. During this period a standard joke circulated among the squadrons, 'I met a Lightning pilot the other day who had flown 40 missions without a fire.'

Another joke doing the rounds was, 'If you want to see a Lightning go to the bottom of the North Sea and wait, if you don't see one go 200 yards in any direction and you can see them wallowing on the bottom.'

One who survived a crash was Flt Lt 'Jim' Wild, his being the twentieth F.6 to crash—on 23 July 1981. XR765, 'Alpha Juliet' of No 5 Sqn took off from Binbrook in the company of a No 11 Sqn F.6 for a Combat Air Patrol (CAP) flown at 3,000 ft (914 m) out over the North Sea off the

*On 3 August 1979 the Lightning celebrated its '25th' with
an impressive display at RAF Binbrook. The station's
painters had plenty of practice on this line-up. F.3 XR751
(No 111 Sqn) nearest, then Nos 92, 74, 56, 29, 23, 19, 11,
and 5 Sqns
(Grimsby Evening Telegraph)*

Yorkshire coast. The two Lightnings were part of Exercise Priory, a major air defence operation.

Once out over the North Sea they came under the control of Staxton Wolds a GCI radar station in Yorkshire. After they had been airborne for about fifteen minutes the two aircraft were vectored behind a Victor tanker.

The No 11 Sqn Lightning made the first contact, while 'Alpha Juliet' remained on patrol in case any targets came through at that critical period while refuelling. 'AJ' remained on CAP and when the other had just about finished he was cleared to refuel, and as the other disengaged from the tanker, XR765 'AJ' started to climb towards the tanker and at about 7,000 ft (2,134 m) had a Reheat One warning—'Jim' Wild carried out the normal procedure and cancelled the warning, checking to see if it was a false. Suddenly another warning sounded and he got the unthinkable—a Reheat Two warning!

Any fire is serious but a Reheat One and Two warning is critical because there are no fire extinguishers in the reheat zone at the back end of the jet pipe where the afterburner is situated.

Seconds were now vital and the pilot immediately put out a Mayday and started to turn for base, continuing upwards at a reduced rate of climb. At that stage the GCI staff alerted all the rescue services and at the same time warned all aircraft in the vicinity to keep away from the area.

Keeping calm and collected and still hoping that the inevitable wouldn't happen, 'Jim' Wild called for another aircraft to check him over from the outside to see if it was a serious warning and if something *was* wrong. But there was no time, for everything started to go haywire as other emergency warnings came on in the cockpit, and at the same time the aircraft began to rock and became uncontrollable. It was the final warning, so the pilot called 'ejecting'. 'I rechecked my straps before pulling the handle—I always strap in tight, really tight—got into the correct posture, pulled the handle and away I went. My impression of it was that I pulled the handle and it seemed like half an hour before the seat fired. This could be misconstrued by people in a situation like this—the seat hasn't gone and they could move at that vital moment of ejection. This happened on the ejection seat rig during practice, people had moved and sustained minor cricks in the neck, but with a full power seat like the one in the Lightning you can have quite a serious back injury.'

Talking two years to the day after the event Flt Lt 'Jim' Wild hasn't had any problem with his back and this was attributed by Martin Baker, who were contacted after the accident, to being correctly strapped in and having the right posture when the handle was pulled.

At the time of ejection the crippled Lightning was at 9,000 ft (2,743 m), travelling at about 200

knots (370 km/h), and another Lightning was now in the area about two miles away coming towards 'Alpha Juliet' and he could see that the aircraft was on fire.

The canopy came away followed immediately by the ejector seat and pilot. His last thought before he pulled the ejection handle was that it was the end of his career and that he would not be able to fly in a fighter again or any aircraft with an ejection seat. If he survived the ejection he may well have sustained injuries which would preclude him from flying again—that was the fleeting thought that flashed through his mind.

He had calmly thought out what he would do, which was to keep perfectly still with his eyes shut while waiting for the automatics to do their job. He had been told that you can get disorientated and experience severe tumbling while in the ejection seat. He would wait with his eyes closed until the parachute opened.

'I ejected just above a cloud layer and when the parachute opened and I opened my eyes I was in the middle of a cloud. What hit me most was the stillness—complete silence—and with being in the middle of a cloud I couldn't see a thing and I presumed that I had gone upstairs to the Almighty or whatever. It wasn't the case and I soon came out of the cloud, and below me a huge patch of boiling, frothing water where my Lightning had smashed into the sea. There was another Lightning in addition to the one that saw me eject, and he was below the cloud being vectored in towards me. He saw "Alpha Juliet"—XR765, hit the sea. With no sign of movement he thought that I was unconscious so he came and had a look. I thought that I was going to get speared by him, but he veered off to avoid being too close.

'During my descent my time was occupied doing the safety drills. I hit the water (which was calm) and got into the dinghy. I had a bit of a problem with the parachute lines which got entangled in my legs and I tried to cut them free, but the knife slipped and nearly punctured the dinghy so I gave up that idea.'

After about 35–40 minutes a Whirlwind helicopter from Leconfield arrived. The downed pilot lit a smoke flare to show the helicopter pilot the wind direction. The winchman then came down and asked if any back injuries etc. and after cutting the parachute lines 'Jim' Wild was hauled into the chopper. As he was being picked up, a Sea King helicopter, which had also been alerted, arrived at the scene and escorted them on their journey to Binbrook. Once aboard he was put near the heater in the Whirlwind to dry off a bit and

during conversation found that the pilot of the Whirlwind was an old friend and they had last met at Leuchars ten years previously.

They landed at Binbrook and were about to depart for a few beers when the MO intervened and had 'Jim' Wild flown to Nocton Hall for X-rays and check-ups. After a night in the hospital Flt Lt Jim Wild was discharged fit and returned to Binbrook. After release from hospital he spent the next 48 hours feeling an elation almost like being drunk, then followed by a bout of depression. This he was assured by the MO was a perfectly normal reaction. After two days it passed and he was back to normal and flying a Lightning.

Flt Lt 'Jim' Wild was just six weeks away from his 41st birthday when he crashed and had done over 2,000 hours on Lightnings. He joined the RAF in 1958 as an instrument mechanic. His ambition was to fly and in 1966 he was commissioned and the following year gained his wings at Syerston. Then after a spell at Valley on Gnats he moved on to Hunters at Chivenor for weapons training, converting to Lightnings at No 226 OCU in October 1969. He was then posted to No 11 Sqn at Leuchars in February 1970 and after two years moved to Binbrook, where he did another two years with No 11 Sqn. He then did a tour with No 92 Sqn at Gütersloh in Germany, staying until the squadron disbanded in 1977. It was then back to the UK, and after a tour with HQ No 11 Group at Bentley Priory returned to Binbrook in August 1979.

Binbrook's Lightning pilots in 'Brown Bear' formation. Wg Cdr 'Mike' Streten, OC No 5 Sqn, is leader. Open day, August 1982 (Grimsby Evening Telegraph)

Chapter 6
Maintenance

The first RAF maintenance unit concerned with Lightnings was No 33 MU at Lyneham, Wiltshire. It was here in 1966 that a most dramatic incident took place with Lightning XM135 which was at the MU in an attempt to diagnose an electrical fault. As the tests did not involve any flying the CO of the MU, who was a technical officer, decided to carry out the tests himself. The tests involved opening up the engines to 85–90% power, releasing the brakes and making a short run along the runway and then closing the throttles. For the test many parts of the Lightning had been removed, including the canopy, and the ejection seat was not armed.

Three test runs were made without incident but on the fourth run the CO accidentally engaged reheat and took off. Fortunately he was a qualified

TOP RIGHT
J/T Ashcroft bleeding the hydraulics of 'AQ' using a rig designed by the Lightning Special Engineering Project Team at Binbrook. 'L SEPTing' takes some 2–3 hours instead of the 2–3 weeks the job would take using normal migration and bleeding

BELOW
Lightning F.6 XS903 of the LTF after a nosewheel collapsed at RAF Coningsby on 14 September 1979

BOTTOM RIGHT
Lightning F.6 XS933 minus engines. Before it returned to No 5 Sqn in December 1982, this aircraft was used as a ground training aid by Saudi personnel at BAe Warton

170

pilot, but he had not flown since 1957. Once airborne he had to try and land, for with the ejection seat not armed he couldn't eject.

After four attempts he managed to land. There can be few who can claim to have had their first jet flying lesson with a first solo and lived to tell the tale.

During 1966, No 33 MU closed down and at the end of the year scrapped XM140, 141, 143, 146, 165, 166 and 167. With the closure of No 33 MU Lightning overhaul and repairs were absorbed by No 60 MU at Leconfield in Yorkshire. Lightnings were also stored at the Lightning Maintenance Unit. The major overhauls and modifications work was carried out by the Lightning Servicing Squadron. No 60 MU had a 'hack' decorated with a golden arrow piercing the nose roundel, giving rise to the aircraft's name 'Golden Arrow' and it was used by the Leconfield Station Flight between July 1967 and May 1968. It then went to Wattisham.

Right from the outset the Lightning gave problems which started at the final and sub-assembly line where there was an inevitable tendency to increase the number of man-hours. The front fuselage, for example, although physically large, was not big enough for more than one man to work in when cockpit equipment, radar, armament and flying controls were being installed. The groundcrews inherited the problems.

Engineering the Lightning

Operating one particular aircraft type from only one airfield makes the engineering effort unique in that all four lines of maintenance are effectively concentrated under one roof. 'First Line' servicing involves the day-to-day replenishments and simple rectification designed to keep the aircraft ready for operation. Second Line comes at the deep scheduled servicing, repairs and modifications in support of first line. Third Line, normally a Maintenance Unit, provides the deep strip, deep repair and storage facilities. Fourth Line is usually the aircraft manufacturer carrying out contracted work—usually a large modification or deep repair. At Binbrook, although all four lines exist, they are often very difficult to clearly identify. For example, the squadrons, normally the first line, carry out some relatively deep scheduled servicing and the various divisions of Engineering Wing overlap in the areas of repair modification and storage. The major elements of engineering the Lightning are divided into four sections—Flight Servicings, Scheduled Servicings, Random Rectification and Modifications. Again, most of the time it is impossible to point to an aircraft and place it in one of these categories. Obviously,

every opportunity is taken during random rectification to carry out scheduled servicing. Let's look at each one in turn.

Flight Servicing—Like any complex mechanical device the Lightning requires fairly constant attention. The flight servicings carried out before flight, between flights (known as a turnround) and after flight concentrate on the replenishment of fuel, oils, air and oxygen. Checking for tyre wear, repacking the braking parachute and checking the security and integrity of the outer surfaces ensures the aircraft is capable of the next flight. These servicings are only valid for a limited time before the replenishments have to be checked again. In particular the thin high-pressure tyres wear very quickly and require replacement every one to ten landings, depending on the weather conditions.

Scheduled Servicing—The Lightning is regularly serviced based on a flying hour cycle of 900 flying hours. This cycle is divided into 75-hour periods. Every 75 hours the aircraft has a Check 1 service. A Check 2 is carried out every 225 hours, a Check 3 at 450 hours and the major servicing at 900 hours is obviously the Check 4. The Check 1 comprises a wash, grease and lubrication with specific items closely inspected. In recent years non-destructive testing (NDT) of various components has been introduced at this check, which entails using magnetic or Eddy current techniques to check for cracking. Because of the early fire problems that dogged the Lightning caused by the design of the fuel and hydraulic pipes which run in the hot zones, extensive fire integrity inspections are now carried

F.3 XP764 during a check 4 service. The Lightning is a labour intensive aeroplane and one airman carries the friend of all mechanics and technicians—a sledgehammer

out on Check 1. The Check 1 takes one to two days to complete. The Check 2 servicing is the first in-depth inspection in the cycle; the engines, and inspection and access panels are removed.

A great proportion of the work involved is now random rectification, although the tasked work is to inspect for faults, wear, corrosion or distortion caused by the previous 225 hours of operation. Check 3s are carried out within Aircraft Servicing Flight—a second-line servicing complex within Engineering Wing. Again the purpose of this 450-hour inspection is to identify any deterioration in

LTF T.5 (XS459/'DX') belly landed in March 1981 and was stored until April 1983. After a check 4 service and repair, the aircraft was restored to full airworthiness

TOP LEFT
Investigating a fuel leak. Aircraft are supported on jacks during major servicing

OPPOSITE
Sgt Farrer checking the wing box structure of F.6 XR771 for fatigue cracks

the integrity of the airframe and components. Many of the components are removed at this stage and inspected in specialist bays. In most cases they are not exclusive to any particular aircraft and become part of a servicing pool. During the Check 3 service the opportunity is taken to repair defects that have been deferred. Often aircraft may develop faults which are acceptable provided they do not deteriorate and are repaired at the next opportunity. Examples of this are minor skin cracks in secondary structure, loss of panel fasteners where there are sufficient left to secure the panel or minor damage to the aircraft which does not affect performance or safety. These defects would be assessed and approved by an experienced engineering officer who defers their repair, in some cases with a proviso that they are regularly inspected to ensure they do not deteriorate any further.

The final inspection in the cycle, the Check 4 carried out at 900 hours, completes the servicing cycle in a similar fashion to the Check 3. At this

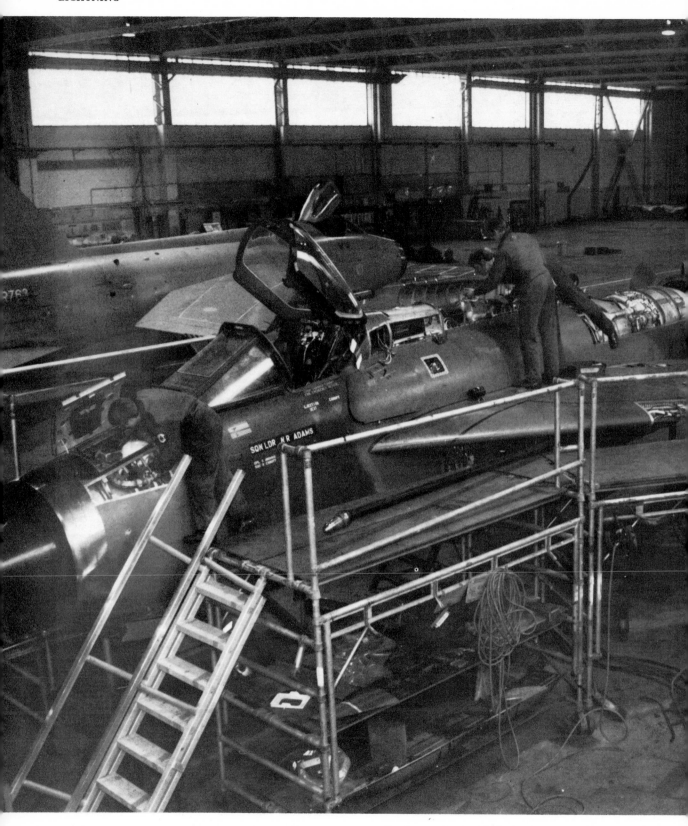

Check 2 service for 'AB'. From left to right: J/T Tunstall disconnecting radar bullet, J/T McAlpine and C/T Caley checking Avpin tank for contamination, Cpl Gray inspecting upper surface of wing (mainplane), and SAC Raynor inspecting leading edge

stage the aircraft is stripped down to its basic structure. Various NDT tests are carried out and most components serviced. The opportunity to improve the aircraft through modification is also taken and all modifications introduced during the cycle are incorporated. The servicing usually culminates in the aircraft being repainted, weighed and balanced in preparation for another 900-flying-hour cycle. A considerable amount of scheduled servicing based on criteria other than flying hours is carried out on the Lightning. Because the major work is flying hour based, the other servicings are known as out-of-phase servicings (OOPS). These include, for example, inspecting the ejection seat every six months (calendar), the brakes every 70 landings; the undercarriage retraction mechanism every 100 retractions; the aileron hinge pin—every hinge pin removed—and various engine components every time the engine hatch is removed.

Random Rectification—By far the greatest amount of work on the Lightning is given to random rectification, that is the repair of components that have failed between scheduled servicings or items that have simply failed and are not a scheduled serviced item. Engine igniter plugs, for example, are not serviced. They are simply tested regularly and replaced when they fail. Complex items like the radar, automatic pilot and engine are more prone to failure and usually create the greatest work for the established hangar rectification teams. The fuel and hydraulic systems on the Lightning are infuriating and prone to leak. Because of the risk of fire considerable energy is expended in ensuring the integrity of these systems. During daily operations the handling or line tradesmen identify and rectify the common failures like tyres and brakes worn to their limits and replacement of fasterners on inspection panels.

Modifications—Following initial production the designers and manufacturers, but in particular the operators and engineers, strive to improve the product and the Lightning is no exception. Also, as the aircraft gets older improvements have to be made to ensure the integrity of the airframe. All these improvements manifest themselves as modifications which can be as simple as replacing a gauge with one that has larger numbers to aid the pilot, right through to adding an additional support beam to the wing joint to reduce the possibility of it fracturing with fatigue. Some 5,000 modifications have been introduced on the Lightning airframe, the latest to improve its strength and subsequently extend the life of the aircraft. Modifications are embodied at all levels depending on their complexity and hence the experience level required.

The Lightning has been in service for nearly thirty years and in that time has been cared for by thousands of technicians. It was not designed with

Four-man team (C/T Couper, Cpl Taylor, J/T Showler, Cpl Stevens), guide the No 2 engine (Avon 301) out of 'DZ', an LTF T.5. Note the FOD bin

SACs Kemp and Clarey at work on the LTF markings worn by 'DZ'. Stencil and spray gun on right

TOP
Lightning F.6 (XR753/'AG') of No 5 Sqn about to raise the temperature at Binbrook with an engine test (check 1). The groundcrew are C/T Wright, Sgt Poskitt, Cpl McCormack, and J/T Fellows

maintainability in mind and is a frustrating aircraft to engineer. The engines have to be removed for access to most ancillary components and to expose the main wing joint. This in itself is a vast servicing penalty made harder by the fact that the latest mark of engine is larger than the original, and has to be fitted to the fuselage with a manoeuvre similar to putting a foot in a shoe. The access panels are small and infrequent compared with modern aircraft. Rumour has it that the designer, having decided the size and location of the access panels on his drawings, then halved their size and moved them all 2 feet to the left. The result is that any Lightning unit has to be manned by dwarfs with six-foot arms. Despite the age of the aeroplane, the difficulties of access and the relative unreliability that causes many hours of overtime and sweat, there is still a great love among those who have worked on it and are still working on it. Perhaps it is the sheer challenge that keeps dedicated groundcrew working on the Lightning.

Fatigue

This is what controls the life of the Lightning and indeed all aeroplanes, not the hours flown. One of the problem areas of managing the Lightning is airframe fatigue. As the end of service date was projected further and further forward the remaining fatigue life of the airframe became a major consideration. A Lightning re-test to gain some 20% more life for this ageing aircraft started in mid-1980, and by running continuously it had overtaken the point at which the original test was terminated by August 1981. The fatigue rig at Warton was used for the tests. Lightning XP697 was used for fatigue tests which were completed on 6 May 1983. Fatigue management plays a big part in extending the life of the Lightning: know the sorties which pile up the fatigue and the ones that don't.

Every aircraft has a Statement of Operating Intent. This is a book which lays down all the profiles that the Lightning would carry out for a war role, and also considers peacetime operations and fatigue.

Monitoring

The RAF uses the Fatigue Index (FI) unit to measure the fatigue damage accumulated by an aircraft. The original design life is allocated a nominal 100 units of FI, (today 130 FI is considered feasible for the Lightning) and every airframe accumulates FI from the day it begins flying. The instrument used to measure FI and monitor fatigue in the RAF is the fatigue meter. This is an accurate accelerometer which clocks up the number of G counts that it experiences in its location near the centre of gravity of the aeroplane. The fatigue meter monitors the day-to-day fatigue consumption and this information is then applied to a formula to establish the amount of FI consumed on each sortie. Fleet fatigue is managed by an executive on the Wing. The Lightning has an RAE Fatigue Meter Mk 14 situated in the fuselage under the right wing. The meter records -1.5 G, -0.5 G, $+0.25$ G, 1.75 G, 2.5 G, 3.5 G, 5.0 G, 7.0 G.

Different types of sorties have very different rates of fatigue consumption. Low-level, high-speed affiliation exercises and air combat manoeuvring against Buccaneer, Jaguar and Harrier aircraft consumes a relatively high proportion of the fatigue life of the airframe. These are the exciting sorties and what a Lightning pilot lives for—very demanding but so exhilarating. Lightnings flying fighter-versus-fighter sorties consume fatigue at six times the average rate. This is the penalty of a sortie with a high manoeuvre content.

As a general rule of thumb, high-speed low-level flying produces up to 10 times more fatigue than a medium- or high-level transit flight. Excessive weight is the most serious consumer of fatigue, because it is akin to pulling G throughout the mission. Adding 250 kg to a Lightning, for instance, reduces the life by 13 per cent. Weight added to the fuselage is worst. Landings are significant too, not just at the moment of touchdown, but particularly when speed has decayed to the point where the wings are no longer lifting. Landing, taxiing, and braking loads all affect the undercarriage.

Fatigue monitoring by means of the fatigue meter depends upon the Fatigue Data Sheet, or MoD Form 725. However, the fatigue meter can only monitor what it experiences and this is confined to vertical G at the aircraft centre of gravity. Before G can be turned into FI, the designer needs to know the weight of the aircraft when the G was applied, the stores configuration, and perhaps the speed, too. Moreover, some parts of the aircraft, like the outer wings, the fin and tailplane, the flaps, airbrake and other components, are affected by stresses other than G and cannot therefore be directly monitored by the fatigue meter. So the designer must estimate the usage of these parts based on the type of sortie. He relies upon his previous experience, and draws on the data given for each mission in the Statement of Operating Intent to arrive at estimates for the unmeasured parameters that govern fatigue consumption during a mission. The RAF fatigue management system is perhaps the tightest and best in the world.

Chapter 7
In-flight refuelling

To extend its endurance the Lightning sprouted a refuelling probe somewhat as an afterthought, attached beneath and extending forward from the port wing; all but the first few production Lightnings were built to accept this probe installation.

Air-to-air refuelling with the Lightning was pioneered by No 56 Sqn at Wattisham and in July 1962 their Lightnings flew non-stop to Akrotiri, Cyprus, with the aid of Valiant tankers.

The Lightnings of No 111 Sqn took part in flight-refuelling compatibility trials with Fleet Air Arm Sea Vixen tankers, and in 1965, No 19 Sqn participated in the proving trials involving the new Victor K.1 flight refuelling tankers. All phases of the trials were successfully completed and pilots from the Lightning squadrons practised the art of flight refuelling in pairs behind the wing pods of a tanker aircraft.

During 1965 Lightning F.3s from No 23 Sqn took part in flight refuelling exercises using USAF KC-135 tankers which had replaced the RAF Valiants that had been hurriedly withdrawn following fatigue problems. The KC-135 filled the gap until sufficient Victor B.1 bombers had been modified for the tanker role. The Victors became available in 1965 as K.1s and K.1As and were based at RAF Marham in Norfolk.

One role of the tanker is to patrol strategic points along the route on long range redeployment flights. The tanker flies a 300 mph (482 km/h) orbit along a 140 mile (225 km) long rectangular track in the sky to await the arrival of the Lightnings. The pilot is calmly talked into position until the probe on the fighter's wing engages the drogue trailing at the rear of the tanker. Two minutes later and 300 Imp gal (1,363 lit) of aviation fuel heavier the Lightning pilot throttles back and drops away to make room for the next. Refuelling a Lightning at more than 300 mph (482 km/h) can be a tricky operation. There is always the big danger of the probe on the Lightning snapping off inside the basket-shaped

The first production Lightning F.1A, XM169, was used for in-flight refuelling trials by the A & AEE from Boscombe Down. Tanker is Vickers Valiant K.1, WZ376

Another view of XM169, this time being refuelled by a specially modified Canberra B.2 operated by the A &AEE

OPPOSITE
Lightning F.6 (XR768/'A') of No 74 Sqn carrying overwing tanks and Red Tops, being 'topped-off' by Handley Page Victor K.1A XH620 of No 55 Sqn. Picture taken late-1960s

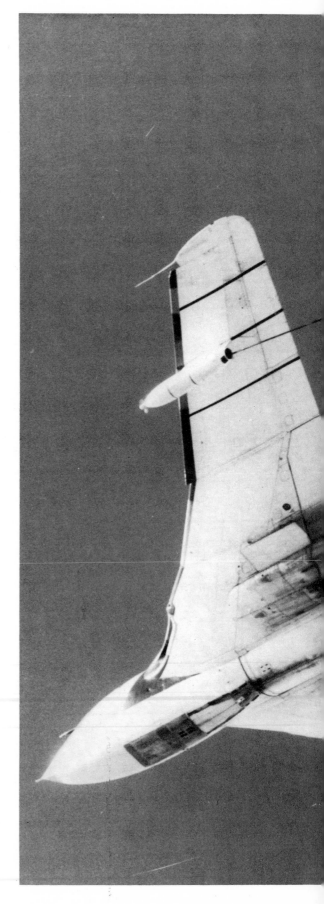

drogue. There could also be drogue malfunctions and any structural failure of the hose or drogue may result in excessive fuel spillage, and the big danger is that the fuel may enter the air intake and cause an engine flame-out.

The tankers are used to extend the endurance of the Lightning on QRA duties to intercept Soviet aircraft. These interceptions usually take place more than 200 miles (321 km) from base. The tanker is a necessity to Britain's airborne watchdogs. As one Lightning pilot put it: 'Know where the tanker should be and find him'.

Joining procedures

Fighter or receiver aircraft always join on the *port* side of the tanker (unless otherwise briefed) and be well forward to be seen by the tanker captain so that he can make a positive identification and call 'in position'. At that stage the tanker captain assumes control of the formation. If other tankers are present they will be in loose echelon on the starboard side.

When the refuelling hoses have been trailed the tanker captain will clear the Lightning to move astern of the hoses. Signal lights, amber, green and red on the refuelling equipment, will show red and amber, indicating that the tanker is not ready for contact. An amber light will indicate the tanker ready for contact and the Lightning pilot should approach the drogue, flying up the line of the hose. The recommended closing speed is at a 'fast walking pace', 3–5 knots, based on the speed at which the tanker hose can automatically wind in after contact. If the contact speed is in excess of 5 knots it is possible for hose-whip to break off the

receiver's probe or, in extreme cases, damage the tanker's refuelling equipment or airframe. Closing speeds cannot be judged from IAS. Therefore, the only way is by the skill of the pilot using visual reference. A 'clunk' will indicate a good contact and when 6 ft (1.8 m) of hose has been pushed in the tanker fuel valves will open, the amber light be replaced by a green, and fuel will flow. If a red light comes on the Lightning must break contact. With any emergency break the fighter pilot must first call 'clear' port and starboard.

If two aircraft join a tanker the second follows the leader at approximately 500 yards (457 m) from about 10 miles (16 km) out. The leader pulls up alongside the tanker with his No 2 in formation at about 30 to 40 yards (27 to 36 m). When both pods are in use the port receiver will be called in once the starboard pilot has plugged in and obtained a green light. The Lightning pilot turns off his radar and selects 'Flight Refuel' to depressurize the tanks. He plugs in by use of formation cues and experience.

The receiving pilot will be informed of the fuel transferred and full contact is maintained until 'clear to break' is heard. When both pods are in use the receivers are instructed to break together— the leader will go to the starboard side of the tanker and his No 2 will follow and formate outside and behind the leader. Both fighter aircraft will then depart from the starboard side, re-calling the controlling agency.

The techniques and procedures for night refuelling differ little from the day procedures. At all times it is important for the fighter pilot to

Boeing KC-135A venting fuel from the drogue at the end of its flying boom immediately after replenishing the tanks of a Lightning F.6

TOP RIGHT
F/O 'Steve' Haskins 'in contact' with Vulcan K.2 of No 50 Sqn at 25,000 ft (7,620 m) over the North Sea. Flt Lt 'Mike' Chatterton, on the port side, has to wait—Vulcan single-point tanker

OPPOSITE
Two Lightning F.6s of No 5 Sqn, piloted by Flt Lts 'Oscar' Wild (starboard) and 'Haggis' Stewart tank-up from a Victor K.2 at 35,000 ft (10,688 m) over the Alps, 29 July 1983

relax as much as possible.

If the case of a silent AAR (for operational reasons or radio failure), the signal lights at the rear of the equipment are used to control the operation. A fighter pilot requiring fuel attracts the tanker pilot's attention and tanker crews are to assume that any fighter appearing alongside the tanker requires fuel and should act accordingly. The tanker acknowledges that he has seen the fighter and understands by means of trailing the tankers hoses by day, and at night by flashing lights three times at intervals of less than one second in addition to trailing the hoses.

No 11 Sqn, equipped with Lightning F.6s at RAF Leuchars, near St Andrews, Fife, Scotland, were flight refuelled to the Far East and back, a distance of 18,500 miles (28,966 km), by aircraft of Strike Command's Victor tanker force drawn from

Nos 55, 57 and 124 Sqns from RAF Marham, near Kings Lynn, Norfolk. The Lightnings flew via Bahrain (a non-stop flight of 4,000 miles (6,437 km)) and Gan in the Indian Ocean, the first aircraft leaving Leuchars on 6 January 1967 and arrived in the Far East two days later.

Over 166,000 Imp gal (754,545 lit) of fuel was transferred from the Victor tankers to the ten Lightnings on the flights to and from the Far East, (sufficient to keep a London bus running for two million miles or four return journeys to the moon). Over 228 air refuelling brackets were made.

Lightning F.3 of No 11 Sqn ready to fill-up from buddy-packed Buccaneer of No 12 Sqn off the north coast of Scotland in February 1982

Now in its twilight years but still as eager as ever, the Lightning's role in overseas deployment has diminished. However, the Lightning squadrons still have regular exchange visits with NATO air forces in Europe and with the French Air Force. Despite its age, the Lightning is still a fighter to be reckoned with.

Abbreviations

A & AEE—Aircraft & Armament Experimental Establishment
AAM—air-to-air missile
ACM—Air Chief Marshal
ADEN—Aden Gun and the name stands for Armament Design Enfield
AFC—Air Force Cross
AFDS—Air Fighting Development Squadron
AIRPASS—Airborne Interception Radar & Pilot's Attack Sight System
ASF—Aircraft Servicing Flight
ASI—Air Speed Indicator
ASSF—Aircraft Storage & Support Flight
AVM—Air Vice Marshal
AAR—Air-to-Air Refuelling
BAC—British Aircraft Corporation
BAe—British Aerospace
BTFF—Binbrook Target Facility Flight

CAS—Chief of Air Staff
Cat—Category
CFE—Central Fighter Establishment

DB—Development Batch
Del—Delivered
Dev—Development
ECM—Electronic Counter Measures
EE—English Electric Company
ETPS—Empire Test Pilot's School

FCTU—Fighter Command Trials Units—Binbrook
FF—First Flight
Flt—Flight

GCI—Ground Controlled Interception

Hittiles—unguided projectile that is designed to actually hit the target
Hz—Hertz

IAF—Interceptor Alert Force
IAS—Indicator Air Speed
lb—pound
IFF—Identification Friend or Foe
ILS—Instrument Landing System
IMC—Instrument Meteorological Conditions
IP—Initial Point

IR—Infrared
IWI—Intercept Weapons Instructor

km—kilometre
km/h—kilometres per hour

LAF—Lightning Augmentation Force
LCS—Lightning Conversion Squadron
LESF—Lightning Engineering Support Flight
lit—litre
LTF—Lightning Training Flight
LTFF—Leuchars Target Facility Flight

Mk—Mark
mm—millimetre
MRG—Master Reference Gyro
MU—Maintenance Unit

nm—Nautical miles
NATO—North Atlantic Treaty Organization

OCU—Operational Conversion Unit

P & EE—Proof & Experiment Establishment
P/O—Pilot Officer
PR—Photographic Reconnaissance

QRA—Quick Reaction Alert

RAAF—Royal Australian Air Force
RAE—Royal Aircraft Establishment
RSAF—Royal Saudi Air Force
R-R—Rolls-Royce Limited
RV—Rendezvous
RWR—Radar Warning Receiver
Sqn Ldr—Squadron Leader
SOC—Struck off Charge
SOTT—School of Technical Training
Sqn—Squadron
SSU—Saudi Support Unit
STCAAME—(pronounced Stickame) Strike Command Air-to-Air Missile Establishment
Stn Flt—Station Flight

TACAN—Tactical Air Navigation
Taceval—Tactical Evaluation
TFF—Target Facility Flight
TSD—Tactical Situation Display

UHF—Ultra High Frequency
USAF—United States Air Force

VHF—Very High Frequency

VMC—Visual Meteorological Conditions

Wg Cdr—Wing Commander
WTFF—Wattisham Target Facility Flight

Lightning F.1A (data applicable to F.1, F.2 and T.4)

Maximum speed	Mach 2.3, 1,500 mph (2,413 km/h)
Length	55 ft 3 in (16.84 m)
Wing span	34 ft 10 in (10.61 m)
Wing area	458 ft^2 (42.70 m^2)
Weights	no data available
Powerplant	Rolls-Royce Avon 210
Thrust	14,430 lb (6,545 kg)
Armament	2 × 30 mm Aden cannon
	2 × Firestreak AAM
	air-to-air rocket packs
Fire control radar	Ferranti Airpass AI.23

Lightning F.3 (data applicable to T.5)

Maximum speed as F.1A	
Dimensions as F.1A	
Maximum weight	approx 42,000 lb (19,050 kg)
Powerplant	Rolls-Royce Avon 301
Thrust	16,300 lb (7,393 kg)
Armament	2 × Firestreak AAM
	2 × Red Top AAM
Fire control radar	Ferranti Airpass AI.23B

Lightning F.6 (data applicable to F.2A)

Maximum speed as F.1A	
Maximum weight	approx 50,000 lb (22,675 kg)
Powerplant	Rolls-Royce Avon 301
Thrust	16,300 lb (7,393 kg)
Armament	2 × 30 mm Aden cannon
	2 × Firestreak AAM
	2 × Red Top AAM
	(F.2A—no Red Top capability)
Fire control radar	Ferranti Airpass AI.23B
	(F.2A – AI.23)

Lightning F.53

Generally as F.6 except Avon 302C turbojets and
AI.23S fire control radar. Also full weapon pack
options, including cameras (see text)

Lightning Crash List

1959
XL628 T.4 1.10.59.
1960
XG334 DB 5.3.60.
XM170 F.1A 2.9.60. XM138 F.1 16.12.60.
1961
XM185 F.1A 28.6.61.
1962
XG332 DB 13.9.62.
XM993 T.4 12.12.62.
1963
XM142 F.1 26.4.63.
XM179 F.1A 6.6.63.
XM186 F.1A 18.7.63.
XG311 DB 31.7.63.
1964
XN723 F.2 25.3.64.
XN785 F.2 27.4.64.
XM187 F.1A .4.64.
XM191 F.1A 9.6.64.
XP704 F.3 28.8.64.
XM134 F.1 11.9.64.
1965
XR712 F.3 26.6.65.
XM966 T.4/T.5 22.7.65.
XP739 F.3 29.9.65.
XG335 DB 1.11.65.
1966
XR721 F.3 5.1.66.
XM190 F.1A 15.3.66.
XM213 F.1A 6.5.66.
XS453 T.5 1.7.66.
XP760 F.3 24.8.66.
1967
XM971 T.4 2.1.67.
XP699 F.3 3.3.67.
55710 T.55 7.3.67.
XM184 F.1A 17.4.67.
XR766 F.6 8.9.67.
XM136 F.1 12.9.67.
XR714 F.3 Cat. 4 27.9.66 soc 16.11.67.
1968
XS900 F.6 24.1.68.
XS924 F.6 29.4.68.
XM188 F.1A 21.6.68.
XS896 F.6 12.9.68.
XM174 F.1A 29.11.68.
1969
XS926 F.6 22.9.69.

1970
XS930 F.6 27.2.70.
XS918 F.6 4.3.70.
XP742 F.3 7.5.70.
XR767 F.6 26.5.70.
XS893 F.6 12.8.70.
XS894 F.6 9.9.70.
XM990 T.4 19.9.70.
1971
XP756 F.3 25.1.71.
XN772 F.2A 28.1.71.
XS938 F.6 4.3.71.
XP744 F.3 11.5.71.
XP752 F.3 20.5.71.
XS902 F.6 26.5.71.
XP705 F.3 8.7.71.
XP736 F.3 22.9.71.
XR764 F.6 30.9.71.
XR711 F.3 29.10.71.
1972
XP698 F.3 16.2.72.
XP747 F.3 16.2.72.
XP700 F.3 7.8.72.
XS455 T.5 6.9.72.
XM974 T.4 14.12.72.
1973
XS934 F.6 3.4.73.
XM988 T.4 5.6.73.
1974
XR715 F.3 13.2.74.
XR748 F.3 24.6.74.
XR768 F.6 29.10.74.
1975
XR762 F.6 14.4.75.
XM991 T.4 .6.75.
1976
XS937 F.6 30.7.76.
1977
XM968 T.4 24.2.77.
1979
XS931 F.6 25.5.79.
XP737 F.3 17.8.79.
XR723 F.6 18.9.79.
1981
XR765 F.6 23.7.81.
1983
XP753 F.3 26.8.83.
1984
XS920 F.6 13.7.84

Lightning Prototypes

P.1A WG760—ff 4.8.54 from Boscombe Down. A & AEE Handling and Performance Trials. Firestreak Trials. The basic aircraft was later fitted with reheat and in 1957 with cambered wing leading edge, a feature to be seen eventually in the F.6/Became 7755M on 2.7.62 for ground instructional use at No 8 SOTT, Weston. 1965 to No 4 SOTT at St Athan/71 MU/RAF Henlow, November 1966/RAF Binbrook 28.7.82.

P.1A WG763 second prototype P.1—ff 18.7.55/A & AEE trials with ventral tank and nose mounted Aden cannon/RAF Bedford 1957 for further flight trials/Allocated 7816M and transferred to Henlow/Manchester Aerospace Museum August 1982.

—WG765—Static Test Airframe only.

P.1B —XA847/ff 4.4.57/Aerodynamic and Repeat Trials with EE and A & AEE. In November 1958 became first British aircraft to reach Mach 2. Two variations of ventral tank were evaluated in mock-up form on XA847, in association with increases in dorsal and ventral fin area./RAE Farnborough/Henlow 1969/RAF Museum Hendon.

—XA853—ff 5.9.57 Aerodynamic and Weapons Development Trials by EE & A & AEE. Withdrawn from use 1964/scrapped at Warton 1965. XA856—ff 3.1.58 Structural Trials with EE/March 1958 to RR Hucknall for Avon engine development/Withdrawn from use 1967/Scrapped 1968.

Lightning production

Development Batch—

One production batch of 20 aircraft built at Warton.

XG307 ff 3.4.58. Aerodynamic and Equipment Development by EE/1964 A & AEE/Withdrawn from use 1970/Scrapped 1971.

XG308 ff 16.5.58. Handling Trials with EE/A & AEE/Fitted with taller, square-cut F.3 fin at Warton in 1964 for trials/June 1966 Aero Flt RAE Bedford. Withdrawn from use in 1968. Scrapped 1968.

XG309 ff 23.6.58. A & AEE early 1960 for gun firing trials/Farnboro/Bedford Farnboro/Scrapped 1967.

XG310 ff 17.7.58. EE for ventral tank jettison and auto ILS trials/A & AEE/converted to prototype F.3 ff 18.11.61 at Warton on it's 212th flight/Aerodynamic and Red Top Trials. Dismantled 1968—fuselage to PEE Foulness.

XG311 ff 20.10.58. First full fuel system. EE, Handling and equipment Development/A & AEE/Tropical trials, Khormaksar, October/November 1961/Crashed into River Ribble near Warton 31.7.63 after u/c failure. Pilot Don Knight ejected safely.

XG312 ff 29.12.58. EE for Development work/Ferranti for A1.23 tests/EE Issued to PEE Foulness 22.7.68.

XG313 ff 2.2.59. Firestreak Tests by de Havilland & A & AEE/To Saudi Arabia as G27-115. Scrapped 1972.

XG325 ff 26.2.59. EE & de Havilland for Firestreak tests/A & AEE/de Havillands for Red Top Development/SOC 23.6.65. Issued to PEE Foulness 7.8.68.

XG326 ff 14.3.59. EE for Red Oxide fuel trials/A & AEE/Warton/issued to PEE Foulness 20.9.68.

XG327 ff 10.4.59. A & AEE/Warton, Fitted F.3 fin by Boulton & Paul/A & AEE/BAC/RAE Bedford/SOC 1970/No 5 SOTT St Athan 1972 as 8188M/Manston April 1977 and used as a pilot rescue trainer.

XG328 ff 18.6.59. EE—equipment & handling tests/A & AEE/BAC and fitted with F.3 fin. Last flight 20.1.66/1968 dismantled prior to issue to PEE Foulness.

XG329 ff 30.4.59. EE. Handling and other trials/Fitted with F.3 fin/A & AEE/de Havilland and used as chase aircraft for TSR-2/A & AEE. To engineering school Cranwell in 1970.

XG330 ff 30.6.59. EE for instrument tests/Fitted with F.3 fin/last flight 5.1.65. Withdrawn from use in 1968—Scrapped.

XG331 ff 14.5.59. EE/de Havilland/A & AEE/tropical trials, Khormaksar, November/December 1961/Fitted with F.3 fin and re-issued to A & AEE/EE and dismantled/to PEE Foulness 4.7.68.

XG332 ff 29.5.59. EE/de Havilland/Crashed on approach to Hatfield 13.9.62. Wreckage to Croydon.

XG333 ff 26.9.59. EE/de Havilland for Firestreak tests/A & AEE/tropical trials, Khormaksar, November/December 1961/Fitted with F.3 fin and re-issued to A & AEE/Warton/withdrawn from use 1968. Scrapped in 1970.

XG334 ff 14.7.59. AFDS—'A' December 1959/Crashed in Norfolk 5.3.60. Wreckage moved to Warton.

XG335 ff 7.8.59. AFDS—'B' December 1959/Warton fitted with F.3 fin/A & AEE/crashed in Wiltshire 11.1.65 after starboard u/c failed to lower. AG335 was on its 286th flight.

XG336 ff 25.8.59. AFDS—'C' December 1959/Warton—fitted with F.3 fin/A & AEE for Red top Trials, September 1965. Last flight on 30.9.68 at Boscombe Down/No 1 SOTT Halton as 8091M/Scrapped 1974.

XG337 ff 5.9.59. A & AEE February 1960/Warton—fitted with F.3 fin/A & AEE for Red Top trials/BAC Warton as target for A1 radar trials/No 2 SOTT Cosford on 27.1.70 as 8056M/RAF Cosford Aerospace Museum.

Lightning F. Mark 1
One production batch of 19 aircraft built at Warton.

XM134 ff 30.10.59./31.3.60 A & AEE/AFDS/74 Squadron 'A'/226 OCU '134'. Crashed in Norfolk 11.9.64.

XM135 ff 14.11.59. 25.5.60 AFDS 'D'/74 Squadron 'R' 'B'/226 OCU '135'/33Mu/Leuchars TFF '135'/60MU—To Duxford for Imperial War Museum 20.11.74.

XM136 ff 1.12. 59.—21.6.60 AFDS/74 Squadron 'S'/EE/74 Squadron 'C'/226 OCU '136'/33MU/WTFF 'B'. Crashed near Coltishall 12.9.67. Pilot ejected safely.

XM137 ff 14.12.59. 28.6.60 AFDS 'F'/74 Squadron 'T'/EE for Mods/74 Squadron 'D'/226OCU '137'/33Mu/FCTU 'Y'/BTFF 'Y'/60MU/BTFF 'Y'/WTFF/5 Squadron 'Y'/60MU/WTFF/60MU for storage. Sold for scrap 16.12.74.

XM138 ff 23.12.59.—30.6.60 AFDS/16.12.60 written off after engine fire on Coltishall's runway.

XM139 ff 12.1.60—2.8.60 74 Squadron 'C'/EE for Mods/74 Squadron 'F'/226 OCU '139'/33Mu for TFF mods/LTFF '139'/WTFF 'A'/Stored at Wattisham 1973. Allocated 8411M used as decoy.

XM140 ff 21.1.60—2.8.60 74 Sqn 'M'/60MU/226 OCU '140'/111 Sqn 'R'/33MU—Scrapped december 1966.

XM141 ff 9.2.60—29.8.60 74 Sqn 'D'/60Mu/226 OCU '141'/33MU. Scrapped December 1966.

XM142 ff 19.2.60—30.8.60 74 Sqn 'B'/crashed 26.4.63 off Cromer, Norfolk. Pilot ejected safely.

XM143 ff 27.2.60—15.9.60 74 Sqn 'A'/60MU/226 OCU '143'/33MU/Scrapped December 1966.

XM144 ff 14.3.60—30.9.60 74 Sqn 'J', 'G'/226 OCU '144'/33MU/60MU/Leconfield Stn Flt/60MU 'Hack' acquiring 'Golden Arrow' paint/WTFF 'B'/60MU/LTFF, '144'/23 Sqn 'X'/74 Sqn 'J' gate guardian at Leuchars.

XM145 ff 18.3.60—8.60 A & AEE/74 Sqn 'Q', 'H'/226 OCU '145'/33MU/LTFF '145'/60MU/Scrapped December 1974.

XM146 ff29.3.60—4.9.60 74 Sqn 'L./60MU/226 OCU, '146'/111 Squadron/33 MU/December 1966 scrapped.

XM147 ff 7.4.60—3.9.60 74 Sqn 'P'/EE for Mods/74 Sqn 'J'/226 OCU '147'/11 Sqn/33 MU/WTFF/'C'/'A' & named Felix the Korky/60MU/WTFF Allocated 8412M and retained for decony duty after TFF disbanded 31.12.73.

XM163 ff 23.4.60—AFDS/74 Sqn 'Q' 'K'/226 OCU '163'/33 MU/WTFF 'A'/60MU/Scrapped December 1974.

XM164 ff 13.6.60—15.7.60 74 Sqn 'K'/EE for Mods/74 Sqn 'L'/226 OCU '164'/33MU/FCTU'Z'/60MU/5 Sqn 'Z'/LTFF/'S', '164'/60MU/Scrapped December 1974.

XM165 ff 30.5.60—29.6.60 74 Sqn 'F'/60MU/226 OCU '165'/33MU/Scrapped December 1966.

XM166 ff 1.7.60—2.8.60 74 Sqn 'G'/60MU/226 OCU '166'/33 MU/Scrapped December 1966.

XM167 ff14.7.60—26.9.60 74 Sqn 'H'/60 MU/226 OCU/'167'/33 MU/Scrapped December 1966.

XM168 Static Test Airframe No number applied. Never Flown.

Lightning F. Mark 1A
One production batch of 28 aircraft built at Warton.

XM169 ff 16.8.60—EE for various trials including radio and flight refuelling/A & AEE/111 Sqn 'B'/33 MU/ 60 MU/TFF 'X', 'B'/5 Sqn 'X'/60 MU/23 Sqn TFF 'W'/Withdrawn from flying duties 31.12.73 and used as decoy at Leuchars.

XM170 ff12.9.60—Written off after first flight at Warton. To 9 SOTT, Newton as 7877M./To fire compound Swinderby 10.66.

XM171 20.9.60—10.11.60 A & AEE/Warton/56 Sqn 'R' 'A'/226 OCU '171'/60 MU/Scrapped July 1974.

XM172 ff 10.10.60—14.12.60 56 Sqn 'S', 'B'/226 OCU '172'/60 MU/226 OCU/from 24.9.74 displayed at Coltishall main gate.

XM173 ff 1.11.60—2.1.61 56 Sqn 'V', 'C'/226 OCU '173'/LTFF '173'/BTFF (11 Sqn)/Approximately December 1976 moved to Bentley Priory and given 74 Sqn marks.

XM174 ff 15.11.60—15.12.60 56 Sqn 'Y', 'D' mid-air collision with XM179 but made a safe landing/226 OCU '174'/LTFF. 29.11.68 crashed near Leuchars. Pilot ejected safely.

XM175 ff 23.11.60—15.12.60 56 Sqn 'T', 'E' withdrawn from active use 2.65/33 MU/60 MU/Scrapped early 1974.

XM176 ff 1.12.60—16.1.61 56 Sqn 'D', 'F' withdrawn from active use 2.65/33 MU/60 MU/Scrapped 8.74.

XM177 ff 20.12.60—28.2.61 56 Sqn 'N', 'G'/226 OCU '177'/60 MU/226 OCU/LTFF '177'/WTFF/LTFF/23 Sqn 'Y'/TFF Duties/WTFF/60 MU/Scrapped 8.74.

XM178 ff 30.12.60—3.2.61 56 Sqn 'O', 'H' Withdrawn from active use 3.65/33 MU/226 OCU '178'/60 MU/LTFF '178'/23 Sqn TFF/Withdrawn from flying after TFF's disbanded 31.12.73 and retained at Leuchars as decoy.

XM179 ff 4.1.61—28.2.61 56 Sqn 'F', 'J'/Destroyed in mid-air collision with XM174 near Wattisham. Pilot injured in ejection.

XM180 ff 23.1.61—8.3.61 56 Sqn 'H', 'K'/226 OCU '180'/60 MU/Withdrawn from active use 6.74. 10.7.74 to Gutersloh as decoy 8424M.

XM181 ff 25.1.61—3.61 56 Sqn 'X'/EE/111 Sqn 'M'/56 Sqn 'L' Withdrawn from active use at Wattisham 4.65 33 MU/60 MU/5 Sqn TFF 'Y'/BTFF '181'. 31.12.73 Withdrawn from active use. Retained at Binbrook as decoy and later to evaluate camouflage.

XM182 ff 6.2.61—13.3.61 56 Sqn 'P', 'M'/226 OCU '182'/60 MU/BTFF/23 Sqn TFF/Withdrawn from active use at 226 OCU in June 1974 and flown to Gutersloh 10.7.74 for decoy purposes.

XM183 ff 9.2.61—6.3.61 56 Sqn 'K', 'N'/33 MU/226 OCU '183'/60 MU/5 Sqn TFF 'X'/60 MU/BTFF '183'/31.12.73 withdrawn from active use. Retained on airfield as decoy.

XM184 ff27.2.61—13.4.61 111 Sqn 'A'/33 MU/226 OCU '184'/60 MU/17.4.67 crashed on landing at Coltishall and written off.

XM185 ff 28.2.61—6.3.61 111 Sqn 'C'/crashed near Wattisham 28.6.61 wreckage to 71 MU, one wing going to Henlow.

XM186 ff 14.3.61—13.4.61 111 Sqn 'B'/18.7.63 crashed at Wittering.

XM187 ff 20.3.61—24.4.61 111 Sqn 'D'/July 1964 u/c collapsed at Wattisham, issued to 9 SOTT Newton as 7838M. By 1978 airframe was at Coningsby for fire practice.

XM188   ff 27.3.61—30.5.61 III Sqn 'F'/226 OCU '188'/33 MU/60 MU/21.6.68 written off. 4.7.68 SOC.

XM189   ff 30.3.61—1.5.61 III Sqn 'E'/226 OCU '189'/60 MU/10.7.74 to Gutersloh for decoy.

XM190   ff1.5.61—20.6.61 III Sqn 'G'/56 Squadron/226 OCU '190'/15.3.66 crashed into North Sea off Cromer. Engine Fire. Pilot ejected safely.

XM191   ff 8.5.61—28.6.61 III Sqn 'H'/9.6.64 written off at Wattisham.

XM192   ff 25.5.61—28.6.61 III Sqn 'K'/226 OCU '192'/60 MU/BTFF 'Z'/WTFF/60 MU/withdrawn from flying 21.12.73. Redecorated in its original scheme as III Sqn 'K' and returned to Wattisham 27.9.74 as gate guardian.

XM213   ff 3.6.61—30.6.61 III Sqn 'L'/56 Sqn/226 OCU '213'/6.5.66 written off at Coltishall when tail hit runway. 11.5.66 SOC.

XM214   ff 29.6.61—1.8.61 III Sqn 'N'/33 MU/226 OCU '214'/60 MU/withdrawn from active OCU use by June 1974. 15.6.74 to Gutersloh for decoy.

XM215   ff 11.7.61—2.8.61 III Sqn 'C'/226 OCU '215'/60 MU withdrawn from active OCU use by June 1974. 14.6.74 to Gütersloh for use as decoy.

XM216   ff 28.7.61—29.8.61 III Sqn 'P' 226 OCU '216'/withdrawn from active OCU use in June 1974. 10.7.74 to Gütersloh for decoy.

Lightning F. Mark 2

One production batch of 44 aircraft built at Warton.

31 converted to F.2A (at Warton from 1966 to 1970).

5 converted to F.52 (at Warton).

The date shown after ff date is the date received for conversion to F.2A the other date is the date despatched.

XN723   ff 11.7.61/A & AEE Boscombe Down/R-R Hucknall for engine development Crashed near Leicester 25.3.64.

XN724   ff 11.9.61. 33 MU/converted to F.2A 20.10.66/19 Sqn 'F' and then scrapped 31.12.76. Decoy at Laarbruch 8513M.

XN725   ff 31.3.62—not converted to F.2A. Used as F.3 prototype with Avon 301 engines and fueldraulic systems fitted/Fitted at Bristol with cambered edges 3.9.63/despatched finally to RAE Bedford for Concorde related noise and speed trials/Scrapped 1.7.71 at Bedford/made 291 flights.

XN726   ff 29.9.61/AFDS 'K'/33 MU/19 Sqn 'D'/19.10.66 conv. F.2A/7 June 1968 92 Sqn 'N'/Farnborough 4.4.77/Foulness 23.11.78.

XN727   ff 13.10.61/19 Sqn 'A'/Conv. F.2A 25.4.69/1.6.70. 92 Squadron 'P', 'W'/Farnboro 4.4.77/To Foulness 20.4.78.

XN728   ff 26.10.61/92 Sqn 'B'/3.4.68 conv. F.2A/24.6.69 92 Sqn 'F', 'V'/RAF Coningsby 6.77 as decoy 8546M.

XN729   ff 3.11.61—AFDS 'L'/33 MU/Warton, Replacement Mk 52 conversion for Saudi Arabia 52-659 FOR-657. Was dev. aircraft Flt. refuel and water cooled pilots suit. Del—Saudi 8.5.67.

XN730   ff 23.11.61/19 Sqn 'B'/4.10.67 Warton conv. F.2A/92 Sqn 'J' 30.8.68/Decoy at Gütersloh, 8496M. To Deutsches Luftwaffen Museum.

XN731   ff 8.1.62/92 Sqn 'L', 'M'/21.3.69 conv. F.2A/92 Sqn 'D' 31.12.69/19 Sqn 'Z'/Reduced to spares/December 1976 decoy Laarbruch, 8518M.

XN732   ff 19.1.62/92 Sqn 'H', 'R'/26.11.68 conv. F.2A/92 Sqn 'R' 12.8.69/Reduced to spares/December 1976 decoy at Laarbruch, 8519M.

XN733   ff 1.2.62/92 Sqn 'L'/19 Sqn 'R'/4.12.68 conv. F.2A/31.12.69 19 Sqn 'Y'/Reduced to spares/December 1976 decoy at Laarbruch, 8520M.

XN734   ff 13.7.62—Warton—used in development programme for F.3. Used for the F.3 300 series engine and the F.3 fueldraulic system/Boscombe Down/Warton 1963/Hucknall on its 158th flight/Warton 1967/Leconfield/Returned to Warton 30.6.73 (322nd flight) and allocated to Saudi School Training aircraft G-27-239 at Warton.

XN735   ff 23.2.62/92 Sqn 'J'/30.8.68 conv. F.2A/25.4.69 19 Sqn 'A'/92 Sqn 'U'/April 1977 scrapped decoy at Wildenrath, 8522M.

XN767   ff 19.2.62/33 MU/Conv. to F. 52 RSAF as 52-655 del. 22.7.66.

XN768   ff 14.3.62/33 MU/92 Sqn 'S'/November 1977 decoy at Gütersloh, 8347M.

XN769   ff 31.3.62/33 MU/92 Sqn 'F', 'Z'/Scrapped December 1973 current RAF West Drayton display.

XN770   ff 24.4.62/33 MU/Removed from storage—conv. to F.52 RSAF as 52-656. Del. 22.7.66.

XN771   ff 29.8.62/AFDS 'M'/33 MU/19 Sqn 'P'/21.9.66 conv. F.2A/21.3.68 19 Sqn 'P'/92 Sqn 'S'/Farnborough/P & EE Foulness 4.78.

XN772   ff 10.5.62/AFDS/33 MU/A & AEE/Rolls Royce/4.9.67 conv. F.2A/2.8.68 92 Sqn 'N' crashed West Germany 28.1.71 spin from 36,000 ft.

XN773   ff 13.6.62/33 MU/Rolls Royce/Leconfield/10.7.67 conv. F.2A/26.6.68 92 Sqn 'E'/Reduced to spares December 1976. Decoy at Laarbruch, 8521M.

XN774   ff 27.9.62/19 Sqn 'C'/13.10.69 conv. F.2A/1.10.70. 92 Sqn 'F'/April 1977 decoy at Coningsby, 8551M.

XN775   ff 1.10.62/19 Sqn 'D'/7.6.68 conv. F.2A/15.1.69 92 Squadron 'B'/Cat 5 fuel leaks decoy at Gütersloh September 1975 8448M.

XN776   ff 18.10.62/19 Sqn 'E'/14.1.69 conv. F.2A/13.8.69 19 Sqn 'C'/92 Sqn 'C'/Decoy at Leuchars, 8537M. Museum of Flight at East Fortune May 1982.

XN777   ff 29.10.62/AFDS 'N'/33 MU/5.10.66 conv. F.2A/26.3.68 19 Sqn 'K'/92 Squadron 'K'/Scrapped April 1977. Decoy at Wildenrath, 8536M.

XN778   ff 9.11.62/9.1.63 19 Sqn 'F'/10.5.68 conv. to F.2A/19.12.68 19 Sqn 'H', 'A'/92 Sqn 'A', King Cobra/Scrapped Wildenwrath 5.4.77—used as decoy.

XN779   ff 22.11.62/19 Sqn 'G', 'X', 'F'/ 60 MU/Spares December 1973 Decoy at Gütersloh.

XN780   ff 7.12.62/19 Sqn 'H'/27.2.68 conv. F.2A/4.10.68 92 Sqn 'K'/19 Sqn 'J'/92 Sqn 'G'/Cat 5 accident at Gütersloh 29.9.75 (ground run fire) and placed out as decoy 8663M.

XN781   ff 12.12.62/19 Sqn 'J'/Warton for conv. to F.2A 13.9.66/26.2.68 19 Sqn 'B'/92 Sqn 'B'/April 1977 decoy at Leuchars 8538M.

XN782   ff 20.12.62/19 Sqn 'K'/26.3.68 Warton for F.2A/25.11.68 92 Sqn 'H'/April 1977 decoy at Wildenwrath, 8539M.

XN783   ff 26.1.63/92 Sqn 'A'/1.5.69 Warton to F.2A/1.6.70 19 Sqn 'G'/Reduced to spares December 1976. Decoy at Bruggen, 8526M.

XN784   ff 26.1.63/19 Sqn 'L'/30.1.69 Warton to F.2A/26.9.69 19 Sqn 'G', 'R'/Scrapped Binbrook 31.3.77. Decoy at Bruggen, 8540M.

XN785   ff 30.1.63/92 Sqn 'C'/Crashed 27.4.64 while attempting to land at the disused Hutton Cranswick airfield (ran out of fuel).

XN786   ff 12.2.63/92 Sqn 'D'/29.10.68 Warton to F.2A/1.7.79 19 Sqn 'M'/Scrapped—ground fire 8.76 to 473 MU Bruggen for battle damage repair techniques. Decoy at Gutersloh, 8500M.

XN787   ff 15.2.63/19 Sqn 'M'/1.7.69 Warton to F.2A/1.6.70 92 Sqn 'L'/Reduced to spares Laarbruch 31.12.76. Decoy at Laarbruch, 8522M.

XN788   ff 25.2.63/Pool aircraft atoLeconfield/92 Sqn 'P'/111 Sqn/92 Sqn 'R'/12.8.69 Warton to F.2A/31.7.70 92 Sqn 'P'/Scrapped Binbrook 31.3.77 Decoy at Bruggen 8543M.

XN789   ff 11.3.63/92 Sqn 'G'/33 MU/5.9.66 Warton to F.2A/3.1.68 19 Sqn 'J'/Reduced to spares 31.12.76. Decoy at Bruggen 8527M.

XN790   ff 20.3.63/92 Sqn 'E'/26.6.68 Warton to F.2A/30.1.69 19 Sqn 'L' Reduced to spares 31.12.76. Decoy at Laarbruch 8523M.

XN791   ff 4.4.63/Pool aircraft at Leconfield/19 Sqn 'P'/21.3.68 Warton conv. to F.2A/29.10.68 92 Sqn 'D'/Reduced to spares 31.12.76. Decoy at Bruggen, 8524M, then for Battle Damage Repair Training.

XN792   ff 18.4.63/92 Sqn 'N'/2.8.68 Warton to F.2A/21.3.69 92 Sqn 'M'/Reduced to spares 31.12.76. Decoy at Bruggen 8525M.

XN793   ff 1.5.63/92 Sqn 'K'/26.9.68 Warton to F.2A/1.5.69 92 Sqn 'A'/19 Sqn 'H'/92 Sqn 'X'/Scrapped April 1977. Decoy at Wildenrath, 8544M.

XN794   ff 16.5.63/33 MU/92 Sqn 'P'/19 Sqn 'W'/60 MU. Decoy at Gütersloh June 1974.

XN795   ff 30.5.63/33 MU/9.7.64 Warton to F.2A/24.9.65 A & AEE/Tornado Cannon Trials and Tornado Flight trials 'chase' aircraft at Warton/P & EE Foulness. Was straight wing aircraft.

XN796   ff 12.7.63/33 MU/Removed from storage. Converted to Mk 52-657 to RSAF Del. 8.7.66. Crashed on take-off 20.9.66. Replaced by XN729—52-659 (May 1967).

XN797   ff 5.9.63/Removed from storage—converted to Mk.52-658 for RSAF Del. Saudi 22.7.66.

Lightning F. Mark 3
One production batch of 63 aircraft built at Warton (excluding XR723 to XR728 and XR747). One converted to F. Mk 53 at Warton. Two converted to F. Mk 6—XP693 and XP697.

XP693   ff 16.6.62 and subsequently used for F.6 development/A & AEE.

XP694   29 Sqn 'D'/56 Sqn 'V'/LTF 'A'/5 Sqn 'R'/60 MU/11 Sqn 'BO'.

XP695   ff 20.6.63/AFDS 'R'—FCTU/60 MU/56 Sqn 'P', 'N'/29 Sqn 'L'/11 Sqn 'O', 'M'/Current Binbrook—Decoy.

XP696   AFDS 'S'/A & AEE/226 OCU/Scrapped Wattisham 1975.

XP697   Converted to Interim F.6—used for trials with the removable multi-purpose tanks on the fuselage underside which was then fitted to F.6 with two slanting stabilizing fins/Warton for stressing—fatigue test complete 6.5.83.

XP698   74 Sqn 'F'/56 Sqn 'T'/29 Sqn 'B'/Crashed in North Sea 16.2.72 after collision with XP747.

XP699   33 MU/56 Sqn 'F', 'O'/Crashed 3.3.67.

XP700   74 Sqn 'A'/56 Sqn 'P'/111 Sqn/'Z'/29 Sqn 'K'/Crashed 7.8.72 in Suffolk.

XP701   29 Sqn 'M'/111 Sqn 'M'/29 Sqn 'F'/56 Sqn 'W'/11 Sqn 'O', 'BN'/

XP702   ff 19.9.63/74 Sqn 'C'/56 Sqn 'R', 'U'/5 Sqn 'P'/11 Sqn 'N', 'BN', 'BO'/Current Binbrook.

XP703   ff 28.9.63/74 Sqn 'G'/56 Sqn 'R', 'S'/29 Sqn 'G'/To Warton for stressing 1975.

XP704   ff 17.10.63/74 Sqn 'H'/crashed 28.8.64 near Leuchars. Pilot killed.

XP705   ff 12.10.63/74 Sqn 'K'/23 Sqn 'K'/29 Sqn 'B', 'L'/Crashed Cyprus 8.7.71.

XP706   ff 26.10.63/74 Sqn 'L'/111 Sqn 'D', 'F'/23 Sqn 'R'/LTF/5 Sqn 'R', 'AR'/11 Sqn 'BM'—current Binbrook.

XP707   ff 13.11.63/23 Sqn 'A'/29 Sqn 'H'/226 OCU/11 Sqn 'BM'/29 Sqn 'F'/current Binbrook.

XP708   ff 19.11.63/23 Sqn 'B'/29 Sqn 'F.N'/P & EE Foulness June 1976.

XP735   23 Sqn 'E'/29 Sqn 'L,J'/Scrapped Leconfield.

XP736   23 Sqn 'F'/29 Sqn 'G'/Crashed in North Sea 22.9.71 killing pilot.

XP737   23 Sqn 'L'/29 Sqn 'J'/226 OCU/11 Sqn 'P', 'N' Crashed in Irish Sea 17.8.79, after u/c problem. Pilot F/O Ray Knowles ejected safely.

XP738   111 Sqn 'G', 'E'/Scrapped at Wattisham 1974.

XP739   33 MU/111 Sqn 'H'/Crashed near Stowmarket 29.9.65.

XP740   ff 1.2.64/226 OCU/111 Sqn 'J,B'/Scrapped at Wattisham 1974.

XP741   ff 4.2.64/111 Sqn 'K', 'D'/5 Sqn 'X'/11 Sqn 'N', 'O', 'BO'/LTF 'DD' Binbrook.

XP742   ff 11.2.64/111 Sqn 'L', 'G'/Crashed North Sea 7.5.70. Pilot ejected.

XP743   56 Sqn 'G'/29 Sqn 'B'/Scrapped Leconfield 1975.

XP744   33 MU/56 Sqn 'H'/Crashed in sea off Cyprus 11.5.71.

XP745   33 MU/56 Sqn 'J'/29 Sqn 'H'/To Boulmer for gate guardian 8453M.

XP746   33 Mu/56 Sqn 'K', 'L'/111 Sqn 'J'/Scrapped at Wattisham 1975.

XP747   33 MU 56 Zqn 'L'/29 Sqn 'S'/Collided with XP 698 over North Sea 16.2.72 and crashed.

XP748   33 MU/56 Sqn 'M'/111 Sqn 'G'/11 Sqn 'P'/Current Gate Guardian at RAF Binbrook 8446M.

XP749   AFDS "T'/111 Sqn 'B', 'K'/LTF 'A', 'DB' Binbrook

XP750   AFDS 'U'/111 Sqn 'H'/23 Sqn 'P'/LTF 'B'/5 Sqn 'Q', 'AQ'/Current Binbrook 'DE'.

XP751   74 Sqn 'B'/23 Sqn 'K,Q'/111 Sqn 'L'/LTF 'C'/5 Sqn 'S', 'AQ'. Current Binbrook.

XP752   74 Sqn 'D'/23 Sqn 'O'/111 Sqn 'Y'/60 MU/111 Sqn 'D'/Collided with a French Air Force Mirage III over France on May 20– 1971/Coltishall fire dump.

XP753   ff 22.5.64/74 Sqn 'J'/111 Sqn 'Y'/56 Sqn 'J'/11 Sqn 'L'/5 Sqn 'X'/11 Sqn 'O' /5 Sqn X, Q, S/LTF 'DC'/Crashed into sea off Scarbrough, Yorkshire, on 26.8.83, killing the pilot, Flt Lt Mike Thompson.

XP754   74 Sqn 'M'/111 Sqn 'X', 'A', 'R'/Loaned to 226 OCU/Scrapped at Wattisham 1975.

XP755   74 Sqn 'P'/56 Sqn 'U'/29 Sqn 'E'/Scrapped Leconfield 1975.

XP756   23 Sqn 'C'/29 Sqn 'K', 'E'/Crashed in North Sea 25.1.71.

XP757   23 Sqn 'G'/29 Sqn 'F', 'M'/Scrapped at Leconfield 1975.

XP758   23 Sqn 'D'/111 Sqn 'S'/29 Sqn 'S'/Scrapped Leconfield 1975.

XP759   23 Sqn 'J'/56 Sqn 'T'/111 Sqn 'G', 'F'/Scrapped at Wattisham 1975.

XP760   23 Sqn 'K'/Crashed 24.8.66.

XP761   23 Sqn 'N'/111 Sqn 'Z', 'N'/11 Sqn 'O,Q'/Allocated 8438M at Binbrook for ground training. To dump end 1982.

XP762   111 Sqn 'M,C'/29 Sqn 'A'/Scrapped Leconfield 1975.

XP763   23 Sqn 'M'/56 Sqn 'K'/29 Sqn 'G', 'P' Scrapped at Wattisham 1975.

XP764   74 Sqn 'H'/29 Sqn 'V,E,C'/5 Sqn 'S'/11 Sqn/'O'/LTF 'B,DB'/5 Sqn 'AR'/current Binbrook ASF.

XP765   56 Sqn 'N'/29 Sqn 'A'/Scrapped at Wattisham 1975.

XR711   ff 3.10.64/111 Sqn 'A'/overshot runway at Wattisham 29.10.71 and placed on dump. Scrapped at Wattisham 1975.

XR712   111 Sqn 'B'/Crashed in sea on way to St Mawgan 26.6.65.

XR713   111 Sqn 'C', 'A'/5 Sqn 'S'/LTF 'S'/11 Sqn 'O'/LAF/5 Sqn 'AR'/current Binbrook.

XR714   111 Sqn 'D'/SOC 16.11.67.

XR715   ff 14.11.64/111 Sqn 'E'/60 MU/29 Sqn 'R'/Crashed 13.2.74 wreck to Farnborough/Scrap Siddal.

XR716   111 Sqn 'F'/226 OCU/56 Sqn 'U'/LTF 'D', 'C'/5 Sqn 'AS'/current Binbrook.

XR717   56 Sqn 'B'/To Boscombe Down Dump 1974.

XR718   56 Sqn 'C'/29 Sqn 'C'/226 OCU/5 Sqn 'S'/LTF 'C'/5 Sqn 'P'/LTF 'B', 'C', 'DC'/11 Sqn/5 Sqn 'AS'/current Binbrook.

XR719   ff January 1965/56 Sqn 'D'/60 MU/111 Sqn 'Z' (loan)/56 Sqn 'Z'/60 MU/226 OCU/1974 on fire dump at Coltishall.

XR720   56 Sqn 'E'/29 Sqn 'L'/11 Sqn 'M'/LTF/11 Sqn 'BN'/LTF 'DA'/current Rinrrok.

XR721   56 Sqn 'F'/Crashed 5.1.66—SOC 13.1.66.

XR722   ff as F.3 23.1.65 Converted to first F.53 for Saudi Arabia 53-666.

XR748   ff (Mk 3) 13.4.65. Del. (Mk 3) 3.2.67. Part converted to F.6 then re-converted to F.3 but with still some Mark 6 modifications on it. 60 MU/111 Sqn 'M'/crashed 24.6.74.

XR749   ff (Mk 3) 30.4.65. Del. (Mk 3) 4.10.67. Part converted to F.6 then re-converted to F.3 but with still some Mark 6 modifications on it. 60 MU/5 Sqn 'Q'/11 Sqn 'BM'/current Binbrook.

XR750   ff (Mk 3) 10.5.65. Del. (Mk 3) 9.10.67. Part converted to F.6 then re-converted to F.3 but with still some Mark 6 modifications on it. 60 MU/56 Sqn 'A'/226 OCU/Scrapped Wattisham 1975.

XR751   ff (Mk 3) 31.5.65. Del. (Mk 3) 16.1.68. Part converted to F.6 then re-converted to F.3 but with still some Mark 6 modifications on it. Last F.3 delivered to Leconfield 16.1.68/226 OCU/29 Sqn 'Q'/LTF 'A', 'DA'/current Binbrook.

Lightning T. Mark 4

One production batch of 21 aircraft built at Warton. 3 prototype + 18 production two—excluding XM967 converted to T. 54 at Filton. XM966 prototype converted to T. 5.

XL628   Company designation P11. Prototype. ff 6.5.59. Crashed into Irish Sea 1.10.59. Test pilot John Squier ejected safely.

XL629   Second Prototype/Empire Test Pilot's School/Retired 3.11.75—Gate Guardian Boscombe Down.

XM966   ff 15.7.60 (Mk 4) First Mk 4 production trainer—converted to T.5 at Filton 1961–62; Second Prototype Mk 5—First Flight as Mk 5 1.12.62; crashed into Irish Sea 22.7.55. Wreckage salvaged.

XM967   T.5 Prototype ff 30.3.62/RAE Farnborough/Honington for disposal in 1974 having flown less than 500 hours/RAF Museum Store at Colerne in January 1975 and allocated 8433M/5 MU Kemble June 1976 and used for fire fighting practice.

XM968   ff 15.7.60/A & AEE/60 MU/226 OCU/92 Sqn 'U', 'Q'/Crashed at Coltishall 13.4.67 repaired. Crashed 24.2.77.

XM969   LCS 'H'/226 OCU/Fire dump at Binbrook 8592M.

XM970   ff 5.5.61. Del. 27.6.62/LCS 'G'/226 OCU/60 MU/19 Sqn 'T'/Brüggen as decoy.

XM971   LCS'K''T'/226 OCU/Crashed in Norfolk 2.1.67.

XM972   LCS 'J'/226 OCU/Waddington fire dump.

XM973   AFDS 'J'/111 Sqn 'T'/23 Sqn 'Z'/226 OCU/19 Sqn 'V'/Brüggen decoy 8528M.

XM974   AFDS 'K'/74 Sqn 'T'/226 OCU/Crashed 14.12.72.

XM987   LCS/226 OCU/Coningsby for Battle Repair Damage.

XM988   19 Sqn 'T'/226 OCU/Crashed 5.6.73.

XM989   56 Sqn 'Z' & 'X'/converted to T.54, 54-650 and later 54-607.

XM990   LCS/226 OCU/Crashed in Norfolk 19.9.70.

XM991   LCS/19 Sqn 'T'/226 OCU/Burnt in ground fire 6/75.

XM992   111 Sqn 'Z'/226 OCU/converted to T.54, 54-651 and later 54-608.

XM993   LCS/overshot runway at Middleton St George and burnt out 12.12.62.

XM994   LCS/226 OCU/71 MU/to dump at West Raynham then scrap in 1977.

XM995   92 Sqn 'T'/to Wildenrath decoy 8542M.

XM996   LCS/226 OCU/60 MU/SOC 18.6.74. Burnt on dump at Machrihanish in 1976.

XM997   LCS/226 OCU/60 MU/Leconfield dump by January 1975 and used by 202 Sqn for winching practice/Catterick and burnt on dump.

Lightning T. Mark 5

One production batch of 22 aircraft built at Warton. Plus XM967 prototype Mk 5. One converted to T. Mk 55 at Filton.

XS416   ff 20.8.64/226 OCU/74 Sqn 'T'/11 Sqn 'T' 'Z'/LTF 'V' 'DU'.

XS417   ff 17.7.64/226 OCU/23 Sqn 'Z'/56 Sqn 'Z'/LTF 'W'/11 Sqn 'T' 'BT'/loan to 5 Sqn /LTF 'DZ'.

XS418   ff 12.11.66/226 OCU/Binbrook Decoy 8531M.

XS419   226 OCU/23 Sqn 'T'/5 Sqn 'T'/LTF 'W' 'DW' 'DV' current Binbrook.

XS420   ff 22.1.65/226 OCU/LTF 'V' 'Y' 'DV'/Storage.

XS421   226 OCU '421'/111 Sqn 'T'/23 Sqn 'S'/Binbrook open storage/A & AEE/P & EE Foulness 27.9.76.

XS422   ff 24.3.65/226 OCU/111 Sqn 'T'/60 MU/29 Sqn 'O'/2T Sqn 226 OCU/ETPS Boscombe Down.

XS423   226 OCU/23 Sqn (loan)/Warton/Decoy at Binbrook 8532M.

XS449   226 OCU/23 Sqn (loan)/Decoy at Binbrook 8533M.

XS450   111 Sqn 'T'/226 OCU/5 Sqn /Decoy at Binbrook 8534M.

XS451   5 Sqn 'T'/T Sqn 226 OCU/11 Sqn 'X'/LTF/RAF St Athan and coded 8503M/RAF Newton 1979 in the Missile Museum.

XS452   226 OCU/29 Sqn 'X'/56 Sqn 'X'/Akrotiri Stn. Flt/11 Sqn 'Y'/LTF/11 Sqn 'T'/LTF 'Z' 'DZ'.

XS453   226 OCU/Crashed 1.7.66 due to Hyd failure.

XS454   226 OCU/11 Sqn 'Y'/Decoy at Binbrook 8535M.

XS455   226 OCU/5 Sqn 'T'/Crashed in North Sea 6.9.72.

XS456   56 Sqn 'A' & 'X'/11 Sqn 'T'/LTF 'T' & 'DT'.

XS457   226 OCU/11 Sqn 'C' Flight 'W'/LTF 'Y'/Boscombe Down 7.79/5 Sqn 'AT'.

XS458   226 OCU/LTF 'Z'/5 Sqn 'T' & 'AT'/11 Sqn 'BT'.

XS459   226 OCU/29 Sqn 'T'/56 Sqn 'X'/LTF 'X' & 'DX' Crash landed at RAF Binbrook 27.3.81. Current at Binbrook.

XS460   Converted to T.55 55-710. Crashed at Warton 7.3.67.

XV328   ff 22.12.66—60 MU/29 Sqn 'Z'/5 Sqn 'T'/LTF 'Y' & 'DY' Current at Binbrook.

XV329   ff 30.12.66 390 MU, Tengah/74 Sqn 'T'/written off after battery acid spillage during shipment from Tengah. Leconfield dump 1974.

Lightning F. Mark 6

One production batch of 62 aircraft built at Warton.

10 Mk3 to Mk 6 Conversions, XR724 to XR747—conversion at Warton.

16 Interim Mk 6 which were returned to works (RTW) for conversion to full Mk 6, XR752 to XR767.

XR723   ff (Mk 3) 2.2.65. Converted from F.3 (2.2.65–9.6.67)/11 Sqn 'L'/23 Sqn 'F'/5 Sqn 'D' 'A'/Crashed 18.9.79—cause engine fire. Pilot, G/Cpt P. Carter ejected safely.

XR724   ff (Mk 3) 10.2.65. Conv. from F.3 (10.2.65–16.6.67)/11 Sqn 'M' & 'K'/LTF 'K'/5 Sqn 'AG' & 'AV'/Current Binbrook.

XR725   ff (Mk 3) 19.2.65. Conv. from F.3 (19.2.65–15.8.67)/23 Sqn 'A'/74 Sqn 'A'/56 Sqn 'P'/5 Sqn 'J'/LTF 'F' & 'DF'/Current Binbrook.

XR726   ff (Mk 3) 26.6.65. Conv. from F.3 (26.6.65–12.7.67)/60 MU Stn Flight/5 Sqn 'N' & 'K' & 'AE'/LTF 'DF'.

XR727   ff (Mk 3) 8.3.65. Conv. from F.3 (8.3.65–15.9.67)/23 Sqn 'F'/11 Sqn 'F' 'G' 'BG'/current Binbrook 'AB'.

XR728   ff (Mk 3) 17.3.65. Conv. from F.3 (17.3.65–1.11.67)/23 Sqn 'D'/56 Sqn 'D' 'J'/LTF 'D'/11 Sqn 'BA'.

XR747   ff (M 3) 2.4.65. Conv. from F.3 (2.4.65–4.1.68)/23 Sqn 'K'/5 Sqn 'P' 'E'/11 Sqn 'BF'.

XR752   First Mk 6 (interim version del. 26.11.65, RTW 20.8.67, Del. Mk 6 20.10.68) FCTU 'V'/Pool aircraft at Leuchars/23 Sqn 'G'/111 Sqn 'Y'/5 Sqn 'B' 'H'/11 Sqn 'D' 'BH'/Repainted grey April 1982—used by 5 Sqn. No cote applied/current Binbrook 'BL'.

XR753   Interim version. Del. 16.11.65. RTW 21.3.68. Del. Mk 6 18.7.69./FCTU 'T' 'U'/23 Sqn 'V'/5 Sqn 'B'/23 Sqn 'A'/5 Sqn 'F' 'A'/11 Sqn 'A' 'BA'/5 Sqn 'AG'.

XR754   Interim version. Del. 3.12.65. RTW 31.1.67. Del. Mk 6 29.2.68./RAF Handling Squadron Boscombe Down/5 Sqn 'G'/23 Sqn 'M' 'D'/5 Sqn 'D'/11 Sqn 'E'/11 Sqn 'A'/5 Sqn 'AE'/current Binbrook.

XR755   Interim version Del. 10.12.65. RTW 7.4.67. Del. Mk 6 23.5.68./5 Sqn 'A' 'O' 'F'/11 Sqn 'J' 'BJ' 'BF' current Binbrook.

XR756   Interim version Del. 10.12.65. RTW 19.4.67. Delivery Mk 6 13.6.68./5 Sqn 'B'/Leuchars Pool 'U'/23 Sqn 'M'/11 Sqn 'J'/5 Sqn 'G'/5 Sqn 'AG'/11 Sqn 'BB'.

XR757   Interim version Del. 21.12.65. RTW 26.1.68. Del. Mk 6 21.2.69./5 Sqn 'C'/23 Sqn 'R' 'V' (No unit markings) 'D'/11 Sqn 'D' 'A'/LAF 'Y'/11 Sqn 'BE'.

XR758   Interim version Del. 11.1.66. RTW. 16.3.67. Del. Mk 6 24.4.68./5 Sqn 'D'/23 Sqn 'E'/5 Sqn 'B'/11 Sqn 'J'/5 Sqn 'E' 'F' 'E' 'AF' 'AH'.

XR759   Interim version Del. 18.1.66. RTW 18.7.67. Del. Mk 6 2.8.68./5 Sqn 'E' 'R' 'A'/56 Sqn 'P'/11 Sqn 'H'/5 Sqn 'H' 'AH'.

XR760   Interim version Del. 27.1.66. RTW 9.1.67. Del. Mk. 6 29.11.67. 5 Sqn 'F'/23 Sqn 'H'/5 Sqn 'G' 'B'/11 Sqn 'BD'/current Binbrook.

XR761   Interim version Del. 15.2.66. RTW 19.1.68. Del. Mk 6 23.10.69. 5 Sqn 'J'/23 Sqn 'P'/56 Sqn 'A'/11 Sqn 'F' 'BF'/5 Sqn 'AC'.

XR762   Interim Version Del. 22.2.66. RTW 16.1.67. Del. Mk 6 29.12.67. 5 Sqn 'K'/23 Sqn 'L'/11 Sqn 'H'/crashed 14.4.75.

XR763   Interim version Del. 11.2.66. RTW 3.1.67. Del. Mk 6 1.11.67. 5 Sqn 'H'/23 Sqn 'G'/11 Sqn 'B' 'E' 'BE'/5 Sqn 'AL' 'AE'.

XR764   Interim version Del. 1.3.66. RTW 23.5.67. Del. Mk 6 12.7.68. 5 Sqn 'L' 'P'/Crashed 30.9.71.

XR765   Interim version Del. 8.3.66. RTW 6.4.67. del. Mk 6 25.3.68. 5 Sqn 'M'—'S' no markings/23 Sqn 'A'/11 Sqn 'C'/5 Sqn 'J' 'AJ'/Crashed off Flamborough Head 23.7.81. Caused by double reheat fire warning Pilot Flt Lt Jim Wild, ejected safely.

XR766   Interim version del. 28.3.66/FCTU/23 Sqn 'T'/Crashed at Leuchars 8.9.67 Cat 5 and SOC.

XR767   Interim version del. 24.7.66. RTW 29.12.67. Del. Mk 6 24.1.69. 23 Sqn 'S'/5 Sqn 'S'/74 Sqn 'E'/crashed 26.5.70.

XR768   First Production F. Mk 6; del. 1.8.66/74 Sqn 'A'/60MU/5 Sqn 'P'/crashed 29.10.74 in North Sea off Mablethorpe. Pilot Flt Lt 'Tex' Jones ejected safely. No 2 engine shut down had reheat fire. Aircraft had done 2129 hours.

XR769   74 Sqn 'B'/A & AEE/11 Sqn 'J' 'B' 'BB' 'BD'.

XR770   74 Sqn 'C'/23 Sqn 'L'/56 Sqn 'D'/5 Sqn 'B' 'A' 'AA'/current Binbrook.

XR771   74 Sqn 'D'/56 Sqn 'C'/5 Sqn 'C' 'AK'/11 Sqn 'BA'/current Binbrook.

XR772   74 Sqn 'E'/5 Sqn 'E'/11 Sqn 'C' 'BB'/current Binbrook.

XR773   74 Sqn 'F'/56 sqn 'N'/5 Sqn 'A' 'B'/11 Sqn 'D'/5 Sqn 'AH' 'AF'.

XS893   74 Sqn 'G'/Crashed at Tengah 12.8.70.

XS894   5 Sqn 'F'/Crashed off Flamborough Head 9.9.70.

XS895   74 Sqn 'H'/5 Sqn 'B'/111 Sqn 'Z'/Leuchars Stn. Flt/5 Sqn 'B' 'AL' 'AK'.

XS896   74 Sqn 'J'/Crashed 12.9.68.

XS897   74 Sqn 'K'/56 Sqn 'S'/11 Sqn 'H' 'BC' 'BD'.

XS898   5 Sqn 'K' 'J'/current Binbrook. Aircraft pulled 10G and overstressed. August 1980 Cat 3 for wing cracks and fuel leaks and then u/c mounting bracket. February 1983 Cat. 3 complete/5 Sqn 'AK'.

XS899   5 Sqn 'G'/23 Sqn 'E'/5 Sqn 'W' 'L' 'C'/11 Sqn 'C' 'BL'/5 Sqn 'AA' 'AJ'.

XS900   5 Sqn 'M'. Crashed 24.1.68 near Leuchars.

XS901   5 Sqn 'D'/56 Sqn 'T'/5 Sqn 'A'/11 Sqn 'G' 'BJ' 'BF' 'BH'.

XS902   5 Sqn 'J' Crashed off Spurn Head 26.5.71.

XS903   5 Sqn 'A' 'C' 'A' 'C'/LTF 'D'/11 Sqn 'BC'/current Binbrook.

XS904   11 Sqn 'A' 'B' 'D' 'BD'/current Binbrook.

XS918   11 Sqn 'B': Crashed 4.3.70.

XS919   BAC for overwing tank trials/11 Sqn 'C'/5 Sqn 'A' 'C' 'A' 'F' 'AD'/current Binbrook.

XS920   74 Sqn 'L'/11 Sqn 'F' 'E' 'B' 'BB'/ Binbrook 5 Sqn/'AF'/crashed at Heuslingen 13.7.84. Believed hit high-tension cables pursuing A-10. Pilot Flt Lt 'Dave' Frost killed.

XS921	74 Sqn 'M'/56 Sqn 'Q'/11 Sqn 'L'/5 Sqn 'H'/11 Sqn 'F'/5 Sqn 'AB'.
XS922	5 Sqn 'H'/56 Sqn 'P'/11 Sqn 'L'/5 Sqn 'A' 'AC'/current Binbrook.
XS923	5 Sqn 'C' 'A' 'C'/11 Sqn 'J' 'BG'
XS924	5 Sqn 'E' Crashed near Beelsby 29.4.68.
XS925	5 Sqn 'L'/11 Sqn 'J'/5 Sqn 'L' 'D' 'AD'.
XS926	5 Sqn 'B' Crashed 22.9.69.
XS927	74 Sqn 'N'/23 Sqn 'O'/5 Sqn 'G'/11 Sqn 'H' 'BH' 'M' 'BH'.
XS928	11 Sqn 'D'/56 Sqn 'E'/5 Sqn 'K' 'L' 'F' 'E' 'F' 'AJ' 'AU'/11 Sqn 'BJ'.
XS929	11 Sqn 'E'/56 Sqn 'L'/11 Sqn 'E' 'BF'/current Binbrook. Had engine fire. Cat. 3.
XS930	11 Sqn 'F'/Crashed 27.2.70.
XS931	11 Sqn 'G'/5 Sqn 'D'. Crashed 25.5.79. Control problems caused pilot, F/O P Coker to eject into North Sea off Hornsea, suffering slight injuries.
XS932	11 Sqn 'H'/56 Sqn 'J' 'R'/5 Sqn 'F'/current Binbrook.
XS933	11 Sqn 'J'/56 Sqn 'K'/5 Sqn 'G'/BAC Warton/Returned Binbrook 16.12.82.
XS934	11 Squadron 'K'/5 Squadron 'J'/56 Squadron 'B'/Crashed 3.4.73.
XS935	23 Sqn 'J'/5 Sqn 'J' 'B' 'AB'/current Binbrook.
XS936	23 Sqn 'B'/11 Sqn 'G'/5 Sqn 'AK' 'AL'/LTF 'DF'/5 Sqn 'DF'.
XS937	23 Sqn 'C'/11 Sqn 'M' 'K'—Crashed 30.7.76. u/c problem. Pilot, Flt Lt S C Manning ejected safely.
XS938	23 Sqn 'E'—Crashed 4.3.71.

Lightning F. Mark 53

One production batch of 46 aircraft built at Warton. 34 to Royal Saudi Air Force, serial 53-667–53-700. 12 to Kuwait Air Force, Serial 53-412–53-423.

Lightning T. Mark 55

One production batch of eight aircraft built at Warton.
6 to Royal Saudi Air Force, serial 55-711–55-716.
2 to Kuwait Air Force, serial 55-410–55-411.

Total Build.

P.1A	....	2 prototypes
P.1B	....	3 prototypes
		20 Development Batch aircraft
F.1	....	19
F.1A	....	28
F.2	....	13 (5 converted to F. Mk 52s)
F.2A	....	31
F.3	....	63
T.4	....	21
T.5	....	23
F.6	....	62
F.53	....	46
T.55	....	8
	Total	339

Acknowledgements

I would like to thank the many people who have given me invaluable assistance during the preparation of this book. Special mention must be given to the Officer Commanding, Royal Air Force Binbrook, Group Captain R L Barcilon, AFC, for allowing me to visit the base about twice a week, and No 5 Sqn for making me most welcome and for plying me with coffee and food—an offer I always accepted unless Wg Cdr 'Mike' Streten was cooking rice risotto! I must also single out the following pilots and groundcrew of Nos 5 and 11 Sqns and the LTF: Sqn Ldr Nigel Adams, Flt Lt 'Chris' Allan, Flt Sgt Les Breach, Flt Sgt Brockleband, Sqn Ldr 'Dave' Carden, Sqn Ldr 'Wally' Hill, Flt Sgt Colin Hillaby, Sqn Ldr 'Jake' Jarron, Sqn Ldr 'Ed' Sowells, Wg Cdr 'Mike' Streten, Wg Cdr Norman Want, Flt Lt John Washington-Smith, Flt Lt 'Jim' Wild and F/O 'Zippy' Zipfell. The following are also notable among those who have assisted:

Aviation News and its editor Alan W Hall for permission to quote from Paul A Jackson's articles in *Scale Aircraft Modelling* Vol 2, No 2, November 1979 and *BAC Lightning Marks 1–16* (Warpaint Series No 2)

The Dennis Baldry Collection

My son Baron

Ken Border

British Aerospace:
Aircraft Group, Warton Division (A F Johnston, Mr Lowe, David Kamiya, John Squier, and Mr Ward)

Charles J Buttigieg

Flight International for material relating to the Lightning, 'Progress with the P.1' (26.4.57) and 'A Day with the P.1' (19.7.57)

Flight Refuelling

Bryan Forway

Neville Franklin

SACW Melanie Goodhall

'The Gun'

Peter Green

Grimsby Evening Telegraph (Pat Otter)

John Jackson

Flt Lt I S Jefferies

Roger Lindsay for permission to quote from *St George's Lightnings* and *The Lightning in RAF Service*

Ministry of Defence:
Air Historical Branch (Air Commodore H A Probert MBE, MA, RAF (TRetd)

Margeret Morris

Maria from Pinnacle Records for the record 'Airline' by Tony Hatch which I played while I wrote this book

Sqn Ldr T G Morris

Jock Pepper

Hans Plantz

Royal Air Force:
Strike Command Public Relations

Stewart Scott

Terry Senior

Sam Smith

SAC Stewart Wastell

Index